MODERN DAY WARRIOR:

A WARRIOR JOURNEY

Rev. James "Seamus" Dillard

GARANUS PUBLISHING

http://www.lulu.com/garanus

Three Cranes Grove, ADF
PO Box 3264
Columbus, OH 43210

Modern Day Warrior

Distributed by The Magical Druid
http://www.magicaldruid.com/
For all your ritual needs!

This book is dedicated to my Grandfather; he taught me the lessons of honor and sacrifice. May I never forget his face.

Table of Contents

Forward

Hello dear reader,

I have been busy reading, writing and organizing notes for this book for about two years. Some of you may have attended my workshops on the subject, and I thank you for your energy, comments and suggestions; it has been (and is) an ongoing journey. The idea for this book came to me when I began re-writing the 1st circle of the ADF Warriors Guild study program. This book is an extension of that program.

I have been a member of the ADF Warriors Guild for about five years and have been on the Council of Honor for about four; in September 2008 I was voted into the office of Guild Chief. This led me to much self-examination and evaluating on what it truly means to be a "warrior" in today's world.

There are many opinions, and we have had healthy debate on the guild email list. I have read book after book on all things warrior. I've reviewed all the old ADF newsletters and guild documents, and I went back and re-read The Solitary Druid by Skip Ellison and all of Ian Corrigan's books and pamphlets, all in an attempt to find the warriors place in ADF.

I've read all the new age spiritual warrior books and fell head long down the corridor of dreams and Jung's archetypes. The thing that resounds most in my soul is that being a warrior is about never settling but constantly striving to better yourself and the world around you. I don't believe all warriors are soldiers, though many soldiers are warriors. I don't believe being a warrior is all about war, though a warrior must be prepared to stand, fight, and even die for their virtues and beliefs. I also hope many of us never have to defend ourselves in a life-threatening situation, but if one arises, we should be prepared.

Being a warrior is not about the military, but we do need to learn from our history books. It is not about security, but we should be ready and know how to protect. It's not about being an Eagle Scout, but we should be able to camp and know our way around in our environment. Being a warrior is about you being the best you. Again, it is about never settling but always striving to improve yourself; mind, body and spirit. Change yourself and you change the world.

The warrior spirit or energy is available to everyone, young or old, male or female, disabled…it's doesn't matter. Tap into that energy of change and improvement. Throughout this book I would like to share with you just a few of the lessons that I learned, and I think you might find them useful whether you consider yourself a warrior or not…

~Seamus

I stand here today not as a Bard,

though I speak from the heart.

Not as a historian,

though I have learned my lessons well.

Not as Seer, though I keep a watchful eye.

Not as clergy, though I offer up my council,

I stand not as a leader, brewer, dancer or healer;

Do not judge me for what I am,

but for what you are.

Without me you could not exist

in the comfort that life affords you.

I am the beacon in the night,

the fire against the cold.

I am what binds the wolf of chaos

and sets things right.

I sacrifice myself for the good of the tribe.

I am a Warrior!

Introduction

I wanted a really cool first line for the book, something like "In the beginning" or my wife's favorite "Since the dawn of time", but I think all the really catchy lines are taken. I guess the best place to start would be at the beginning (I tried starting at the end but it didn't work).

First, I should explain some of the things I talked about in the foreword. What are ADF and its Warriors Guild? So much of this book comes from that perspective, and I think it's important for anyone reading this to understand that first and foremost this grew from a spiritual place.

So what is ADF? Isaac Bonewits, author, ADF founder and Archdruid Emeritus wrote

"The Irish words Ár nDraíocht Féin, pronounced 'arn ree-ocht fane,' means 'Our Own Druidism,' and that's just what ADF is - a completely independent tradition of Neopagan Druidism. Like our sisters and brothers in the other Neopagan movements, we're polytheistic Nature worshipers, attempting to revive the best aspects of the paleopagan faiths of our Ancestors within a modern scientific, artistic, ecological and holistic context. Like our predecessors and namesakes, the Druids, we're people who believe in excellence—physically, intellectually, artistically and spiritually.

"We're researching and expanding sound modern scholarship about the ancient Celts and other Indo-European peoples in order to reconstruct what the Old Religions of

Europe really were. We're working on the development of genuine artistic skills in composition and presentation. We're designing and performing competent magical and religious ceremonies to change ourselves and the world we live in. We're adapting the polytheologies and customs of both the Indo-European Paleopagans and the Neopagan traditions that have been created over the last fifty years. We're creating a nonsexist, nonracist, organic, and open religion to practice as a way of life and to hand on to our grandchildren. And we're integrating ecological awareness, alternative healing arts, and psychic development into our daily activities. Together, we're sparking the next major phase in the evolution of Neopaganism and planting seeds for generations to come." (adf.org/about)

ADF has many sub-groups within the organization. We have local congregations or "Groves." There are also "Kins" based on cultural focus and "Guilds" and "SIGs" (special interest groups). Here is what is listed on our website:

Artisans Guild: creating and promoting training in the making of artworks and crafts

Bardic Guild: promoting excellence in the word: spoken, written, and sung

Brewers Guild: promoting and sharing knowledge of the art of brewing in a religious context

Dance Guild: exploring performance and research of dance and movement in Our Druidry

Healers Guild: studying, practicing, and teaching a variety of healing arts

Liturgists Guild: promoting the art and science of liturgy within the context of Our Druidry

Scholars Guild: practicing scientific and scholarly research on the roots of Our Druidry

Magicians Guild: studying, practicing and teaching the traditional arts called magic

Naturalists Guild: learning more about the land we live on and its Nature Spirits

Seers Guild: training and fellowship in the skills of divining, trancework, and counseling

Warriors Guild: training in spiritual, mental and physical defense, also emergency response

(adf.org/about)

The Warriors Guild mission statement is:

The ADF Warriors Guild exists to serve ADF with members who are trained in spiritual, mental and physical defense, designing & performing liturgy for Warrior spirituality, and emergency response.

Hopefully everyone now has a better idea of my starting point on this path, as I have stated this book expands upon the work I did to develop the guild's study program. I didn't do the work alone. Guild members and ADF members from all over have added their valuable input. To all those who stood around the fire at festivals or huddled up in Guild meetings and to the warriors on the guild email list I say: THANK YOU!

There are a few people I would like to thank personally so here goes that honor role...

- **Rev. Mike Dangler,** for allowing my own voice to develop in ADF, for being a friend, a priest and an example (even when it was a bad one) [link to his site]
- **Rev. Kirk Thomas,** for insights, opinions and thought provoking discussions Woof! [link to his site]
- **Rev. Jenni and Missy,** for proof reading and editing. Me no write good!
- **Nora, Jessie, Awen, Jon, Faolan and others** who always had great ideas and opinions.
- **To my Crane-kins!** Three Cranes Grove rocks! [link to 3CG]
- **To Ian, Skip, Isaac and others** who walked before us and beat back the undergrowth so that we have an easier path to walk.
- **To the Council of Honor** – Donagh, Selene, and Orion. For all the work each of you has done to help me with this and all things Warriors Guild! I love you guys!
- Last and so most importantly, **to my wife,** for everything she does. To Leesa, My Warrior!

"So it is that good warriors take their ground on solid ground where they cannot lose, and do not overlook conditions that make an opponent prone to defeat."

~Sun Tzu – The Art of War

"Search others for their virtues, thyself for thy vices."

~Benjamin Franklin

Chapter 1

Know Thyself

As in any successful enterprise, we should lay the groundwork for our future success. The overarching theme of this book will be the **Warrior Way** and how we incorporate this philosophy into our daily lives. The Warrior Way is an adaptation (really, a continuation) of the Druid Triad introduced in "Our Own Druidry" (the ADF Dedicant Program). There, Ian Corrigan writes, "Druidry is a religion of the mind, of the heart and of the flesh." Taking this same concept into the warriors' realm, we see that the triad of three becomes: body, mind and soul. The path then is broken up into these three areas of focus: physical, mental and spiritual. As warriors we must strive to constantly improve ourselves in these three disciplines. It is by challenging ourselves to improve and be the best we can be that we tap into the energy and essence of the warrior

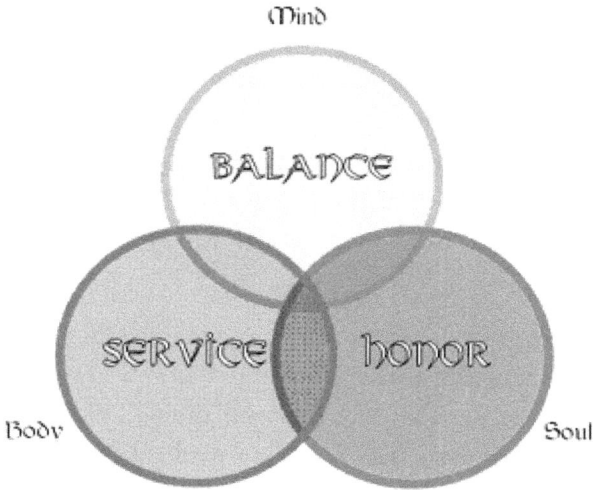

As you will see, the triad will become multi-layered with meaning as we travel the path. This layered triad is the Warrior Way. Honor, balance and service should be the three key elements of the warrior's outlook and lifestyle. By focusing on these three qualities, we will expand and deepen our understanding of the warrior's role in today's society.

The Warrior Way

- **Honor -** There can be no path for the warrior without honor. The warrior does what is right, no matter the ease or the cost. We must sacrifice ego for right action. There is no hope for balance without honor.
- **Balance -** The warrior strives for balance in all endeavors. We must be in harmony with the energy of the universe.
- **Service -** The warrior places others and their welfare above his own. The warrior's role in society is to serve

their family/community, the Kindred and themselves. There are great rewards in service. As you give, so do you receive.

These three guiding principles should be the foundation of your work. In all endeavors, look to make sure that you hold to these core values. The Warrior Way is not always an easy path, but it is one that is full of blessings for those with the courage to walk it.

Since we are discussing guiding principles, let us review ADF's Nine Virtues for those who might not be familiar with them and how the Warrior Way fits with them. This is my take on the virtues; ADF asks that everyone explore and form their own understanding of the virtues. The Warrior Way works with any set of virtues or with any religion, this just happens to be my path.

My virtues

Since I first began my first draft of my DP work way back when, I have really tried to live these virtues, and the closer I get to them, the more fulfilling my life has become. It is a great reality check to check yourself against these virtues. These virtues have become my code of conduct that I review to ensure that I am a reflection of my beliefs and that I walk my path. I have included honor here separately to show the difference between honor and integrity, but in my life, I see them as outward and inward manifestations of the same virtuous behavior.

Courage

"Courage is rightly esteemed the first of the human qualities because…it is the quality that guarantees all others."

~Sir Winston Churchill

n. - The state or quality of mind or spirit that enables one to face danger, fear, or vicissitudes with self-possession, confidence, and resolution; bravery

We start with courage. Why? Because courage is the virtue that holds all the other virtues together. If you do not have the courage to stand by your convictions, then what is your worth? We must have the courage to stand beside our virtues and our fellowship. Many of us live in the world where our courage isn't road tested. I hope that if I am truly faced with a life threatening danger I will have the courage to face it, to look it in the eyes and deal with it. I think I do.

From the warrior's perspective, courage is a product of self-control, discipline and knowledge. When faced with a danger, you must assess the situation and, using self-control and discipline, find the best course of action to attack the situation. Knowledge about the situation and the possible outcomes should weigh into your reaction. However, you still need the courage to react or act. One should not be reckless but act with the speed and economy of force needed to overcome the issue. Not all problems or dangers we face are physical; there is a need for moral courage. I would think that it is easier to be courageous if you have an untroubled conscience. If you believe in what you are doing, if you have the confidence of past victories and the discipline to do what is required, then courage should be a by-product of preparedness and belief in oneself.

Relations:
- **Kindred:** Shining Ones
- **Hallow:** Fire
- **Color:** Red

- **Realm:** Sky

Honor

"A man has honor if he holds himself to a course of conduct because of a conviction that it is in the general interest, even though he is well aware that it may lead to inconvenience, personal loss, or grave personal risk."

~Brigadier General Marshall, The Armed Forces Officer

n. - 1. High respect, as that shown for special merit; esteem: the honor shown to a Nobel laureate. 2. a. Good name; reputation. b. A source or cause of credit: was an honor to the profession. 3. a. Glory or recognition; distinction. b. A mark, token, or gesture of respect or distinction: the place of honor at the table. c. A military decoration.

If courage is the virtue that holds all the other virtues together, then honor is the workhorse that guides them, day in and out. Could you be a virtuous person without honor? Honor, to me, is the legacy that you build though your words and deeds. It is the outward manifestation of your honesty and integrity.

For one to walk with honor they must be humbled before the Kindreds. You must give respect (honor) to the kindred and be a living example of your virtues.

I am a Tyrsman, and to be honorable is to walk upright, to be a steward of the community and to be right acting for not just your personal honor but also that of the community. Every time someone meets me or sees me, I want them to walk away knowing I am an honorable man. I strive to be good example of an ADF druid and not a hypocrite.

Integrity

"False words are not only evil in themselves, but they infect the soul with evil."

~Socrates

n. - 1. Steadfast adherence to a strict moral or ethical code. 2. The state of being unimpaired; soundness. 3. The quality or condition of being whole or undivided; completeness.

Integrity is what is needed to walk in honor. Honor is the legacy that good thought, good deeds and good words build. Integrity is the tool that one uses when building that legacy.

It is the internal moral compass that shows you right from wrong. One must have integrity when faced with temptation. It is that conscience that tells you to do right—not because of fear of being caught, but because it is the right thing to do.

Acting with integrity is often a road of personal hardship. It means taking a stand or committing to an idea of what is right.

Integrity is personal: what one feels is right or just others might disagree with. Honor is more tangible, cultural.

Relations:
- **Kindred:** Ancestors
- **Hallow:** Well
- **Color:** Blue
- **Realm:** Sea

Wisdom

"One's first step in wisdom is to question everything – and one's last is to come to terms with everything."

~Georg Christoph Lichtenberg

n. - 1. The ability to discern or judge what is true, right, or lasting; insight. 2. Common sense; good judgment: "It is a characteristic of wisdom not to do desperate things" (Henry David Thoreau). 3. a. The sum of learning through the ages; knowledge: "In those homely sayings was couched the collective wisdom of generations" (Maya Angelou). b. Wise teachings of the ancient sages. 4. A wise outlook, plan, or course of action

Wisdom is the combination of knowledge and intuitive knowing and knowing how you apply it. There are book smarts, street smarts, common sense and then those things that some people just "get".

Some people just look at a car engine and it makes sense; some people just sit down at a piano and start to play at it with a certain aptitude. This may be a genetic knowledge of information imprinted on the mind from a past life.

Then there is book smarts learned in school oftentimes by repetition. Moreover, there are street smarts: what you need to pick up for survival.

Lastly, there is common sense, which is intuitive understanding. All these are forms of knowledge, and wisdom is the combination of these and how and when to use them.

Knowing something is of little value if you do not know how to apply that knowledge to your life. That is not wisdom that is trivia. Wisdom is also the ability to reason things out to a conclusion.

Relations:
- **Kindred:** Ancestors
- **Hallow:** Well
- **Color:** Blue
- **Realm:** Sea

Vision

"Life has no other discipline to impose, if we would but realize it, than to accept life unquestioningly. Everything we shut our eyes to, everything we run away from, everything we deny, denigrate, or despise, serves to defeat us in the end. What seems nasty, painful, evil, can become a source of beauty, joy, and strength, if faced with an open mind. Every moment is a golden one for him who has the vision to recognize it as such."

~Henry Miller

n. - 1. a. The faculty of sight; eyesight: poor vision. b. Something that is or has been seen. 2. Unusual competence in discernment or perception; intelligent foresight: a leader of vision. 3. The manner in which one sees or conceives of something. 4. A mental image produced by the imagination. 5. The mystical experience of seeing as if with the eyes the supernatural or a supernatural being.

What is wisdom without vision? Vision could mean many things. Our vision is obstructed and shaped by where we are in life. The classic saying about 20/20 hindsight is a very true statement. We often have better vision looking back from a distance. You lose perspective sometimes when you are too close to an issue or situation.

So, what is vision? The ability to see things for what they are or to see things for what they can be? Vision, I think, is both.

Certainly, people talk about someone having vision when they can see the potential of something. Then there is the act of having visions and tapping into the spirit world. Trancing or meditation can lead to a vision. Furthermore, there are those among us with a "six sense," an ability to sense a future happening. Reading runes, telling fortunes—types of vision.

Vision is personal. I will always see things differently than a truly tall person or a female or a black man, things that shape my worldview are different from theirs. People see things differently depending upon their personal history, experiences and circumstances.

Relations:
- **Kindred:** Shining Ones
- **Hallow:** Fire
- **Color:** Red
- **Realm:** Sky

Moderation

"Moderation is a fatal thing. Nothing succeeds like excess."

~Oscar Wilde

adj. - 1. Being within reasonable limits; not excessive or extreme: a moderate price. 2. Not violent or subject to extremes; mild or calm; temperate: a moderate climate. 3. a. Of medium or average quantity or extent. b. Of limited or average quality; mediocre.

I do not totally agree with moderation as it is thrown around in ADF and in life.

Moderation seems to imply giving 50%, not truly living life or pushing yourself out of your comfort zone to grow. I am not talking about hurting yourself or others; that would be ignoring the other virtues. What I think we should be striving for is balance. Balance is a necessary part of a Warrior's life.

The military sometimes uses the term "economy of force," meaning use only as much as necessary to complete your objective. Though I understand the concept, it seems to suggest complacency in life dressed up as a virtue, and that is a waste. If we look at moderation as a statistical average, it could mean living life to the extremes, and over time, it would still balance itself out to moderation. Live life - don't watch it.

Relation:
- **Kindred:** Nature Spirits
- **Hallow:** Tree
- **Color:** Green
- **Realm:** Land

Perseverance

"Courage and perseverance have a magical talisman, before which difficulties disappear and obstacles vanish into air."

~John Quincy Adams

n. - 1. Steady persistence in adhering to a course of action, a belief, or a purpose; steadfastness.

Perseverance is the ability to just keep going even when all signs say, "stop." I felt this virtue the most a few Wellspring Festivals ago during the Warrior's Circle Challenge.

I was a late entry, added to even up the brackets and was in no real shape to fight. I went through all five rounds with two fights having draws that went into bonus rounds, three minutes each. The last round for the win was awful. I was sucking wind and having leg cramps. The mind wanted to do so many things, but my body just wasn't able!

At that point, I had nothing to lose but I could not quit. Something clicked in my mind, and I just knew it would not be fair to the other fighter and most importantly, to me. I never wanted to look back and think "what if?"

We must carry our flag every day. In weightlifting, true gains are made right there on the other side of giving up. We often find we do have that "little extra" if we push just a little more. If we believe in what we are doing, then what other option do we have but to see it through?

Relation:
- **Kindred:** Ancestors
- **Hallow:** Well
- **Color:** Blue
- **Realm:** Sea

Piety

"Piety is not a goal but a means to attain through the purest peace of mind the highest culture."

~Johann Wolfgang Von Goethe

n. - 1. The state or quality of being pious, especially: a. Religious devotion and reverence to God. b. Devotion and reverence to parents and family: filial piety. 2. A devout act, thought, or statement.

The act itself is piety. Every time you do ritual, meditate or do some kind of devotional, it is an act of piety.

It is through doing these acts, that you build the relationship with the three kindred or the deity to whom you are praying.

When you have the discipline to be pious, to put your energy and focus into the act, that is when you make the act sacred.

Is going through the motions to get to the sacred separate from the sacred itself? I don't think so; we have a Core Order of Ritual for a reason. Maybe this is why so many things that are religious or spiritual are universal to all walks of life. We connect to those things which have had reverence paid to them over time. They have been made sacred.

So being pious is the act, the doing, even when you don't feel like it. Fake it 'til you make it, because you truly do make it.

Relation:
- **Kindred:** Shining Ones
- **Hallow:** Fire
- **Color:** Red
- **Realm:** Sky

Fertility

"A mind without instruction can no more bear fruit than can a field, however fertile, without cultivation."

~Cicero

adj. - a. Capable of initiating, sustaining, or supporting reproduction. b. Capable of growing and developing; able to mature: a fertile egg. c. Highly or continuously productive; prolific: a fertile imagination; a fertile source of new ideas.

When we stop learning and growing, we have reached the apex of life and begin to die. We must continue to be productive and creative or we become stagnant. It seems to me that most of us have that need for personal growth and development.

I have this need to have an open mind, always looking for new things to ponder and an open heart, always looking for new experiences to enjoy. Fertility of the soul for me has always been making of music. There is something about taking words out of the wind, writing them down and arranging them to a rhyming pattern and then adding music to it and bringing this idea to life. That creative process is making magic. That is an act of fertility.

Relation:
- **Kindred:** Land Spirits
- **Hallow:** Tree
- **Color:** Green
- **Realm:** Land

Hospitality

"There is no beautifier of complexion, or form, or behavior, like the wish to scatter joy and not pain around us. 'Tis good to give a stranger a meal, or a night's lodging. 'Tis better to be hospitable to his good meaning and thought, and give courage to a companion. We must be as courteous to a man as we are to a picture, which we are willing to give the advantage of a good light."

~Ralph Waldo Emerson

n. - a. The friendly reception and treatment of guest or strangers. b. The quality or disposition of receiving and treating guest and strangers in a warm, friendly, generous way.

Open you door and your heart. Since joining ADF, Leesa and I have met so many wonderful people and had the pleasure to have many of them over to our house for meetings, rituals, fellowship and laughter.

We have had some west coast people stay the night before and after festivals, and the time spent with them enriched our lives and served to deepen our relationships. This extends to our grove, too.

There is something great about making people feel welcome and extending that treatment to them. It really displays to the world your other virtues. What is the point of the other eight virtues if you're not willing to share them, or to lend a hand to those who need it?

When I think of this virtue, I think of a lonely figure walking through the blinding snow with head down low. The figure is stumbling and tired and cold, but through the sleet in the distance is a house with smoke drifting out of the chimney and firelight glowing through the window…how could you not open your door and share your bread and hot tea?

Relation:
- **Kindred:** Land Spirits
- **Hallow:** Tree
- **Color:** Green
- **Realm:** Land

Deepening These Virutes, and Other Virute Systems

These are my interpretation of the ADF virtues. They are not the only virtues one could live by; we see other examples in the Nine Noble Heathen Virtues and in other religious systems:

in Wicca, there is the Wiccan Rede; in Buddhism, there are the Four Noble truths, etc. The Warrior Way can be adapted to work with any of these religious systems.

The ADF virtues can be broken down as such within the Warrior Way:

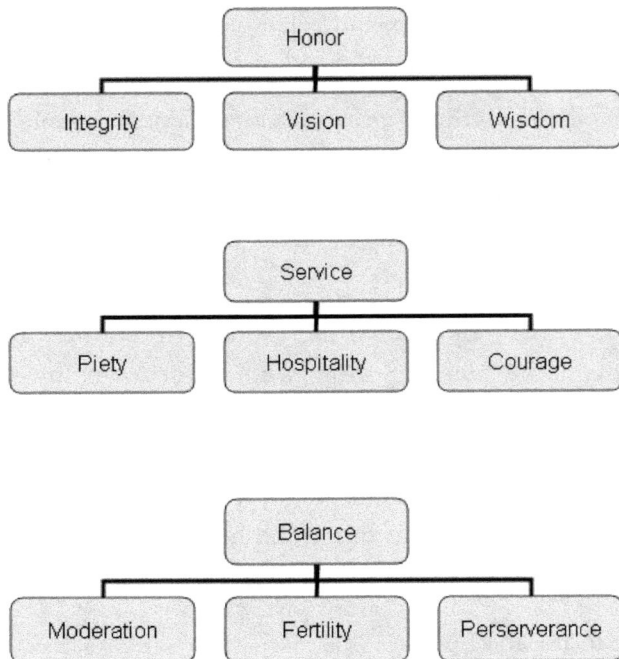

```
                    ┌──────────────┐
                    │    Honor     │
                    └──────────────┘
        ┌──────────────────┼──────────────────┐
┌──────────────┐   ┌──────────────┐   ┌──────────────┐
│   Integrity  │   │    Vision    │   │    Wisdom    │
└──────────────┘   └──────────────┘   └──────────────┘


                    ┌──────────────┐
                    │   Service    │
                    └──────────────┘
        ┌──────────────────┼──────────────────┐
┌──────────────┐   ┌──────────────┐   ┌──────────────┐
│    Piety     │   │ Hospitality  │   │   Courage    │
└──────────────┘   └──────────────┘   └──────────────┘


                    ┌──────────────┐
                    │   Balance    │
                    └──────────────┘
        ┌──────────────────┼──────────────────┐
┌──────────────┐   ┌──────────────┐   ┌──────────────┐
│  Moderation  │   │  Fertility   │   │ Perserverance│
└──────────────┘   └──────────────┘   └──────────────┘
```

This is the foundation to begin your path following ADF's virtues. For those who are Wiccan or follow a Native American Path I have sketched out a similar Warrior Way.

Wiccan Virtues
- **East** - Vision, Piety
- **South** - Courage, Transformation
- **West** - Wisdom, Integrity
- **North** - Fertility, Hospitality
- **Center** - Moderation, Perseverance

Native American Virtues
- **East** - Eagle or Hawk
- **South** - Coyote or Phoenix
- **West** - Salmon or Whale
- **North** - Buffalo or Stagg
- **Center** - Grandfather or Great Spirit

Assignment 1

Sit down and review your personal virtues, your own core values, and think about how they guild you in your life. If you had to sum up your life and how you live it, would it be a reflection of your virtues? Write this reflection down. I firmly suggest grabbing a notebook and start keeping a journal as you work through the remainder of this work.

Use the ADF virtues, the 9 noble virtues that other groups like The Troth use or come up with your own 6 to 9 virtues that really call to you. Research these virtues and write down your understanding of them. As yourself, what they mean to you? Think of them as your private bylaws for how you are going to live your life.

"Lack of activity destroys the good condition of every human being, while movement and methodical physical exercise save it and preserve it."

~Plato

Chapter 2

Warrior Health

This section will review what you need to do to push yourself physically. For the exercises I have outlined I have consulted a friend of mine, Brent Saunders. Brent is an ACE certified trainer. I thank him for his advice, time, energy and friendship.

For reference to the nutrition side of the chapter, I worked for GNC for the several years and have completed the company's intensive product training as well as online study programs through the University of Florida.

As in all new physical endeavors, I advise you to consult with your doctor before beginning any exercise program. The purpose of this chapter is to help the warrior engage in health-oriented, moderate, non-professional physical activity on a regular basis.

The warrior is expected to find and regularly engage in a non-job-related physical activity with the intention of health improvement and stress release.

Basic Exercise Programs

Beginner's basic Routine:

(Three days a week, M/W/F, etc)

As a general overview, each exercise should include 2 warm up sets with light weight to get the blood pumping to the area and warm up the muscles (about 25% of your maximum lift).

After warm up you will do what is known as a "pyramid set:" You will start with about 40% of your maximum lifting weight and move up to about 85% of your maximum weight. The "pyramid" comes into play as you add weight: begin with a lighter weight with a higher number of repetitions (reps), and as you add weight, decrease the number of reps. Then, work your way back down, lightening the weight and doing more reps. As a target for weight amount, you want to use enough weight to make the last rep of each set difficult. You also want to wait 60-to-90 seconds between sets to allow for muscle recovery. Make sure you drink plenty of water!

Day one: Legs
  1. **Leg Press**
     - 2 warm up sets- 15 reps
     - 1st set 40% MW 12 reps
     - 2nd set 60% MW 10 reps
     - 3rd set 75% MW 8 reps
     - 4th set 85/90% MW 6 reps
     - 5th set 75% MW 8 reps
     - 6th set 60% MW 10 reps
     - 7th set 40% MW 12 reps
  2. **Leg Curl**
     - Same as above except no warm up set needed
  3. **Calf Raises (standing or seated)**
     - Same as above – 1 set warm up

Don't push yourself too hard the first couple of times or you will not be able to walk much for the next couple of days. As you get into the routine, your body will get used to it, but you may still feel tender a day or so after a work-out. This is known as DOMS (Delayed Onset Muscle Soreness) and most experts say it is due to lactic acid build up.

Day two: Back and Biceps

Lat Pull Down (arms about shoulder with apart sit about slightly back and pull the bar to chest level, think about trying to get shoulder blades to meet in the middle of your back)

1. **Lat Pull Down**
    - 2 warm up sets- 15 reps
    - 1st set 40% MW 12 reps
    - 2nd set 60% MW 10 reps
    - 3rd set 75% MW 8 reps
    - 4th set 85/90% MW 6 reps
    - 5th set 75% MW 8 reps
    - 6th set 60% MW 10 reps
    - 7th set 40% MW 12 reps

When you exercise your back you also use your biceps, because of this your biceps have all ready been warmed up so you can now bicep curls.

2. **Bicep Curls**
    - Same as above

Day Three: Chest and Triceps
1. **Bench Press**
    - 2 warm up sets- 15 reps
    - 1st set 40% MW 12 reps
    - 2nd set 60% MW 10 reps
    - 3rd set 75% MW 8 reps
    - 4th set 85/90% MW 6 reps

- 5th set 75% MW 8 reps
- 6th set 60% MW 10 reps
- 7th set 40% MW 12 reps

2. **Tricep Pull-down** (I prefer rope and I like it when at the bottom of the pull you twist your hands so that your thumbs go from side by side to facing the ground)
   - Same as above

This is a very basic starting point. Over time, you may want to pull in more exercises from any of a variety of sources. For example, you may wish to add leg squats or lunges. You could do bent over rows or cable rows to exercise your back, but please make sure you keep your back straight and use your upper back area to perform the exercise. You may want to get a personal trainer for a session or two just to show you proper movement. There are hundreds of books, DVDs and magazines to help you mix it up and illustrate proper technique so that you don't hurt yourself.

You should also jog, bike, row, etc, to get your aerobic exercise. Some people do aerobic exercise the same day as weight lifting, others on non-work out days. If you are trying to lose weight I suggest you workout first thing in the morning on an empty stomach. This will speed up your metabolism and help burn fat as energy.

Finally, keep in mind that you need to stretch after you work out, too. It will help prevent soreness and stiffness.

Diet

Now, let's take a few minutes to take about diet and nutrition. First of all, anyone who knows me knows I carry around a little extra weight. This is one of my personal disappointments and a source of constant frustration. I come from a long line of big boned, sturdy...fat people. Anyone who has seen me in the Warrior Circle Challenge knows that I still move well! Overall, I am a healthy fat person that at the age of 40 plus has nothing in his medicine cabinet but pain reliever and vitamins. It is all about being healthy! I know so many people that struggle with their self image, whether fat, skinny, pear-shaped, big butt, small breast, double-chin, big nose....we all have our issues. The idea here is to make positive changes in yourself and walk in balance. The following is just some very basic nutritional information. Refer to the back of the book for some great books to help you along the way.

Nutrition can be as easy or difficult as you make it. "Good nutrition is the foundation of good health. Everyone needs the four basic nutrients – water, carbohydrates, protein and fats – as well as vitamins, minerals and other micronutrients." (Balch 3) It really is as simple as that. Eat balanced meals that consist of proteins, carbs, and fats; take a multi-vitamin and drink 8 glasses of water daily.

A balanced meal does not mean how many plates you can balance on your walk back from the buffet bar. Most of us in the US eat too much. Too much at one sitting, too much processed foods, too much fast food, too much fat, too much salt, too much fried...we have sold our health for convenience. (Yes I said WE, now pass me my number 4 value meal.)

The easiest thing for all of us to do would be to eat more greens, more complex carbs, and less fatty foods, less simple carbs. My chiropractor, Dr Jay, offered me the easiest suggestion I have ever heard: When you fix your plate start with your protein source (chicken, steak, pork-chop etc) and add your green-beans and mashed potatoes (whatever your side dishes are) and eat one bite protein, one bite veggie (green-bean),and one bite starch (potato); when your meat is gone then you are done. Think about it for a minute, we usually eat two to three times the carbs than we do the protein. Even diet is about balance!

I would also stress serving sizes when discussing eating habits. Eat servings that are the size of your fist or a deck of cards. If you need to eat more often throughout the day but eat smaller serving sizes, it will not only help aid digestion, but more of the foods you eat will be used for energy—and less converted to stored energy (i.e. FAT).

I could go on and on, but that is not the purpose of this book. I would like to mention alcohol and other substances. I, for one, have been known to lift a horn in ritual or around the fire, but as a warrior you should remember balance sometimes IS about moderation. Anything that you do that leads to self destruction is bad. Seek help for addictions and remember we all have dragons to slay.

Lastly I would suggest a cleansing program that one could do a couple of times a year to help change the oil and clean your filters…I mean if it's good enough for your car?

Assignment 2

Keep a four-month journal of activity(ies) and recap of changes to your body weight, measurements and stamina. Reflect on how working out made you feel. Did it change you spiritually? Help your stress, etc?

"The sword conquered for a while, but the spirit conquers forever!"

~Sholem Asch

Chapter 3

Daily Devotionals

First things first...Since I have made mention of the Three Kindred, let's begin with a more in-depth look at who they are. Again, this is my view. Spend some time with them yourself and learn who they are to you.

My Kindreds

To begin, start with the following prayer. You should have an offering for each of the Three Kindreds: the Ancestors, the Nature Spirits, and the Deities. Cornmeal is a good choice. Light a candle and spread the offering onto the ground where the prayer indicates.

The Daily Offering Rite

I make offering

and ask my ancestors to walk with me.

Those of blood and bone,

those of spirit and faith,

Those who have blazed the trails before me so that I may walk easier,

I praise and thank you.

Hail the Ancestors.

[Offering made]

Nature Spirits, walk with me

today and always,

Thank you for your lessons

and sacrifices.

To the tree, I give offerings and ask my Nature Spirits

Those of stone and soil,

tree and leaf, blood and bone,

Those who dance the spiral dance with me so that I may walk in balance,

I praise and thank you.

Hail the Nature Spirits

[Offering made]

Shining Ones, walk with me

today and always,

Thank you for your wisdom

and blessings.

To the fire, I give offerings and ask my Shining Ones

Those of my grove, those of my hearth, and those of my heart.

You who light the way with your brilliance, may I walk my virtues.

I praise and thank you.

Hail the Shining Ones

[Offering made]

To the Kindred three,

For all the blessings I thank thee

May my voice resound in the well.

May my voice echo

through the trees.

May my voice carry on the fire.

I stand before you Mighty, Noble, Ancient Ones,

Not broken or on bent knee

But standing tall and free.

Thankful for the blessings

you have given me.

May I walk in honor, balance,

and service

May my actions be just,

My thoughts pure.

Hail and glory to the Kindred

A gift for a gift, I have offered you praise and offerings. Now I ask of you, Mighty, Noble Ones

What lessons do you have for me?

[Pull omen, (see next chapter)]

I thank the Kindreds for their blessings and wisdom. May I walk in Honor, Balance and Service, so be it.

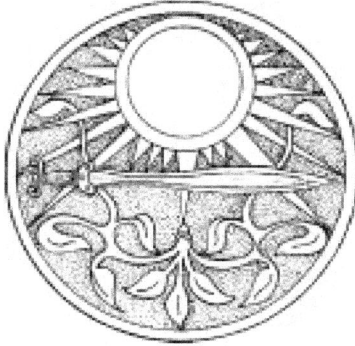

The Ancestors

I start with the Ancestors because all that I am is because of them. Every step of the journey of my people has led to me.

This is a tremendous responsibility that I must carry with me. I think of all the untold tragedy and hardships that my family encountered throughout the years and survived all leading up to me, just for me to take my place in line, not first, not last, but as a steward of my lineage.

I think of my great grandfathers swimming in the Rhine, fighting in the plains and hills of Europe. Of the Elliot clan fighting and revving across the Scottish borders. I think of my great grandmothers tending the soil of the land and fighting the cold, long, hard winters, and the fight for survival. I think of the open skies and the night by firelight. I think of my grandmothers and grandfathers of North America and the coming of the white man. I think of the ever-changing landscape of my ancestors as they journey through time.

I pull my thoughts closer to my beloved great-grandfather that I had the privilege of knowing and sitting with until I was ten. I recall all the stories he told me of the days that passed before his eyes, of my grandparents all now part of the Star –Nation. I pray to my Gods that I never forget the faces of my fathers or mothers and that I listen to the voices that whisper in my heart.

Think of your ancestors of blood and bone reaching back through time, all those who suffered through hardship. What a burden of responsibility we carry with us. All that they did, all that they suffered, all their joys and sorrows were cogs in the wheel of life that has carried them to us. So we here we stand, a testament to their perseverance. With each step we take we must remember to honor their memory.

We must also remember that we, too, are cogs leading to the next generation and what we do prepares the world for them and their place in line. We are beholden to the past and the future.

Daily/Weekly Meditations

It has been said that meditation is an effective way of reducing stress and helping teach you to relax both mind and body. Meditation is an exercise that can also help build self-esteem and self-discipline, but like all exercises you must work at it to get better. There are many different types of meditation exercises you can do, here are two examples.

First is a simple meditation that I picked up while working on my ADF Dedicant Program. I'm not sure where I adapted it from but it was probably Ian Corrigan, so I credit him if not for the meditation itself then as the inspiration for it.

Find somewhere to sit down that is comfortable and quite. Sit down and relax. If it helps stretch before you begin, and some may wish to record the meditation so they can listen to it instead of read it. If you do yoga then that would be a great time to work this meditation as well. Once you are ready, sit and breathe...

The Warrior Meditation

Listen to your breathing, quiet your mind, think of your thoughts as background noise on a radio and turn them down. Listen to your body, feel your body.

Take inventory of yourself, relaxing, breathing deep, in....out...in...out. Feel the weight of your arms as they sit folded in your lap or hanging by your sides...

Breathe in deeply and hold it for a second; then slowly exhale...slowly and completely. Breathe in and out, feel your legs and feet and wiggle your toes...

Take another deep breath, and hold it before slowly releasing it...ahhhhhhh.

Feel you heartbeat, listen to the soft beating that courses the blood through your body...

Relax and feel that rhythm. Roll your neck and relax, allow your body to go deeper...relaxing and listening to your own breathing...again take a deep breath...hold it....and slowly release, it pushing at the end until all the breath is out...

Now in your minds-eye, imagine a seaside...paint a picture in your mind of waves as they gently flow onto the beach and then just as easily recede back out...

Hear that sound of the surf...that gentle whooshing sound of the waves as they meet the sand...

Hear the sound of birds and smell the salt in the air...continue to breathe deep...in and out...

Feel the wind and sun on your face...allow yourself to enjoy the moment...feel the warmth of the sun, relax and just breath...

Allow your cares to flow away on the waves...in and out like your breathing...as the waves take your troubles and concerns, feel the wind blow away doubt and negativity. Breathe deep and relax, be at ease with yourself...

The sunlight that warms your face penetrates you and energizes you. Warms you to the core...let that warmth wash over you...now just be...sitting there, relaxed, energized...

When you are ready, once again breathe deep and release it slowly...feel yourself coming back into your body...into the here and now, once again feel the weight of your legs...your arms...open your eyes and feel how relaxed and at peace you are.

Try this meditation exercise or write one of your own. You could use a setting of the forest, a meadow, a winter afternoon, a fall day, whatever helps you.

* * * * *

I know that some people cannot sit still but find they can get into a meditative state while jogging, others love to put headphones on and listen to drum or trance-type music. You need to find what works for you, but there is a magic in learning to be still. There are other meditations in the book so if this one did not speak to you and you can't seem to write one yourself try one of the other ones. Don't give up! Focusing yourself is hard, more for some than others, but keep trying and you will be surprised at how much easier it gets the more often you do it.

Assignment 3

Begin doing the warrior meditation at least three times a week and try doing a daily prayer or devotional. Review these tasks and your reflections for a three month period. How do you feel? Has meditation become a part of your life?

Also include those of heart kin, adopted families, grove and community ancestors. We also honor the Ancestors in the form of the Ancient Wise; the Druids, Bards and Wise Ones of old. In a warrior setting this would also include Warriors and Heroes of myth, lore and history.

Ancestor worship is not new or uniquely ADF, and it can be found as a rather large component in many contemporary pagan religions. Asatru' practices are heavy into ancestor worship. The Alfar and Disir are worshiped during 12th night. The Celts and most modern day pagans celebrate Samhain as The Day of the Dead and make sacrifices to the Ancestors.

Walk into any home and look at the photos and keepsakes of the dearly departed and it becomes clear that regardless of religious leanings or cultural background, we all practice some form of ancestor worship.

The Nature Spirits

Next are the Nature Spirits, the Landvaettir, my brothers and sisters on this plane, all those beings who walk with us and share the Mother, those ancient ones who will teach us the lessons of existence in this realm. Some Nature Spirits are our allies and come to us as totems to teach and to guild us along our journey. They might also be our house plants and pets. Others might be those things that go bump in the night. They are the wild and untamed creatures of stone and rock, tree and fig, fur and feather.

Nature Spirits are also the faerie folk, brownies or housewights.

Why is that we humans feel the need to lord over things, to live outside of the natural cycle and rhythm of things? I sometimes think of us as the cancer of the world. We destroy and rip trees and dirt and entire ecosystems apart so that we might have yet another shopping mall. I feel that there is a great hurt that we are inflecting upon our mother. If we just slowed down and listen to the whispers in the wind, we could hear the nature spirits crying out.

The numbers of endangered or extinct animals and green kin are staggering, and yet we blindly continue on (more on this later).

We must remember that we do not live outside the sacred spiral but within it. We must all remember to walk gently and try to leave the lightest of footprints. We share this world with the spirits of nature.

One of the problems in modern society is we tend to think we are above nature, that it is something to control, something over which we hold dominion. We are oftentimes out of balance with the world around us. I feel one of our biggest opportunities as "druids" or "warriors" is for us to be good stewards of the land that surrounds and supports us.

Again worship of the Nature Spirits is nothing new. In fact, it may have been the beginning of religion. We have always been dependant on nature. Whether it was the hunters and gathers that prepared for the hunt by enacting a ritual of the hunt, or the early settlers who tilled the land and prayed for rain, or sunshine. Remember the first shamans who could predict an animal's behavior by their waste, and the first priest or druids who could predict the weather or change of seasons?

All neopagan religion is nature- based in some way. The accepted neopagan holiday calendar is based on the cycles of nature.

The Shining ones

Last but first, the Shining Ones, those Matrons and Patrons who shine down their blessings to us daily, those that guide and nurture us: The Deities.

"First children of our Mother, oldest and brightest; Gods and Goddesses of ancient times" is a standard refrain in ADF liturgy. It is the Shining Ones that we read about in our myths and legends, our greatest heroes and first ancestors. They are deities of sky, storm and sun, deities of sea, field and forest, of moon, river and hearth. When most people think of praying, it is to these beings that our prayers are directed.

In addition, ADF members, unlike some other pagan groups, think of each deity as separate and unique instead of just an attribute or interpretation of one cosmic "Lord and Lady."

"Each Pagan culture has a family of deities whose wisdom, love and power sustain the worlds and humankind. Whether these cultural forms portray separate, individual entities; or whether they are names and titles of

one great family of gods and goddesses, they are the object of our highest worship, and are our greatest allies"

~Our Own Druidy, p. 26.

The Shining Ones represent different parts of me. I have Norse leanings which call to me in myth and attitude. I also have the Celtic influences that I see as interrelated to the Norse path, not just as Indo-Europeans but in my personal ancestry. I pray to the Shining Ones for wisdom and for blessings of health and happiness.

In my worship of the Gods and Goddesses, I find that regardless of who you pray to or what path you follow, it is the act of piety that enriches your life. The spiritual growth comes in the action, over time it builds and resonates in your life and in your heart.

The more I give to the Kindreds, the more I receive in return, the more I hear their voices in my mind and feel their presence in my soul. The closer I get to them, the more closely I come to the vision of what it means to be a druid. Self-actualization is the top of Maslo's pyramid of hierarchy...the closer I walk with the Kindreds the closer I am to self-actualization.

As the standard ADF liturgy states each time we give to the Kindreds they grow stronger as do we...

Assignment 4

Now that you have a basic understanding of the Three Kindred, take a few moments to reflect on your feelings about each of them and record your thoughts in your journal. If you have already done this for ADF then record your thoughts on how each of these Kindred relate to being a warrior. Think of which Shining Ones would make a good matron or patron for a warrior. Which would you call on for strength or protection? Which ancestor or hero might you seek out to mentor you on your warrior path? Which animal ally would you call on to help you on your journey? If you have a totem or animal ally already, how do they help you as a warrior?

Daily Devotionals: Piety in Practice

The following pages contain examples of daily devotionals, prayers and mediations to get you started with a habitual devotional schedule.

Although I admittedly don't spend as much time as I would like in meditation, I can say that I always feel better after I do the work. Getting into the habit of doing devotionals or setting aside time for meditation and prayer and actually doing it is what piety is all about. Piety is performing the spiritual actions, whether we feel like it or not, and building relationships with the Kindred whom we honor.

There are many techniques for meditation and trancework to be explored, but what I offer you here are some basic works to get you started with Warrior spirituality. It is my hope that you will develop your own as you learn and grow based on your own experiences and those Deities, Ancestors and Nature Spirits with whom you walk on your path.

Warrior's Morning Prayer

Hail the Shinning Ones

Thank you for your blessings

Please continue to watch over me

May I walk in Blessings!

Hail the Ancestors

Thank you for your sacrifice

Please continue to guide me

May I walk in honor!

Hail the Land Spirits

Thank you for your lessons

Please continue to teach me

May I walk in balance!

Today is a good day and I stand as a warrior

Ready for the call of duty

I walk in blessings, honor and balance

If today is my last day then may I die as I walk:

In blessings, honor and balance

Daily Devotional

      I do this is the morning, so I don't do a full grounding and centering, but a simple focusing where I raise my hands palm up to around my chin as I inhale and then push my hands back down, palms down as I exhale nine times. This is known as the Nine breaths.

For those you of that are ADF members I never do outdwellers at home due to both respect for my housewights and the warders of our house, Thor and Brigit. I call to Garanus (Crane) as my gatekeeper and animal ally, but you can call any gatekeeper you wish. I also don't do the ADF full order of ritual for my daily devotionals.

The Devotional

I call out to Garanus, Mighty Crane

Walker between the worlds,

beholden to none

Totem guild, grove mate

One foot on land, one in the water, with your head raised to the sky

Join your magic with mine, ward and aid me as I walk through this day.

[Offering made]

First, I thank the Mother Earth

All that I am and all that I have

Is because of her

She cradles me in her bosom

She clothes me,

feeds me and keeps me

May I walk softly

and leave light foot prints

[Offering made]

Ancestors, walk with me today

and always,

Thank you for your lessons

and sacrifices.

To the well, I give

"So what is appropriately performed sacred ritual? Very simply, it is a symbolic enactment with a spiritual focus that is performed by an individual or a group of people. Ritual is a process whereby we may connect with consciousness -with spirit, through the heart, using the psychic tools of invocation, symbol, symbolic action and clear intention"

~Sivananda Math

Chapter 4

ABC of Rituals

Now that you have some daily piety and meditation happening in your life, it might be time to introduce more full-blown rituals. I have a few rituals here for a solitary warrior to do at the hearth. Later in the book I will introduce group ritual and working with a "lodge."

So, what is ritual? A ritual act is one that is routine, a habitual repetitive event or series of events. Everyone has rituals. Many of us have morning rituals to help us begin our day. For me it is get up, go to the bathroom, shave, shower, eat breakfast, and drink my second cup of coffee while reading the sports page. It is surprising how that simple morning routine or ritual affects my day. If for any reason it is disrupted I find myself out of sorts that day.

But what about ritual in a spiritual sense? Why do we do what we do? In the context of this book, we will assume the question is referring to religious rituals, in particular, ADF style rituals.

Dictionary.com defines ritual as; "prescribed, established, or ceremonial acts or features collectively, as in religious services or an established or prescribed procedure for a religious or other rite." Regardless of religion (or lack thereof), all ritual has a very similar purpose. Simply stated, it is an act or a series of acts which help those participating in the ritual to reach a desired end-point. The group of acts are merely road signs to help us find our way to the desired results.

So no matter how we dress it up, ritual is a reoccurring pattern or set of acts that help us achieve a desire result.

Listed below are some of those functions in no particular order. The following list is a composite list from several sources, including books or articles from Ian Corrigan, Isaac Bonewits and Kerr Cuhulain. For the purpose of citations, I will use Ian Corrigan, but this in no way infers that the list or work is his alone or that it was original.

To connect with the divine or supernatural.

The intent is to establish or strengthen the ties/relationships we have with those to whom we are praying/sacrificing (God(s), Kindreds, etc). Think of it as meeting a friend for lunch every week. As you develop a relationship with that friend, that relationship strengthens over time and deepens with the shared memories. Now think of distant friends that you see in social situations maybe yearly. The relationship of the weekly lunch friend is more intimate and richer than that of a mere acquaintance

To serve the Kindreds.

I'm not sure how much needs to be said here. Piety is a must in any spiritual/religious endeavor

To attain spiritual fulfillment of those who attended the rite.

Once that relationship is established with the divine then worship should be fulfilling to all the participants

To strengthen the bonds of unity and community.

There is an old saying that "the family that prays together, stays together." There is truth to the community building that worshiping together provides. Sharing sacred space and opening oneself to working with energy is a shared experience unlike any other.

Growth for the ritual performers/writers.

Piety is in the doing. I know that for my grove, the more we work together and share ritual space the more comfortable we are together and the more our voices blend into the chorus that is "our" worship. Ritual, like many things, gets better with practice. We have gotten to the point that we are no longer reading from scripts but speaking from the heart with a shared vocabulary

Rites of occasions (Holidays, weekly/monthly/daily devotions, rites of passage, energy work.

This one really needs no explanation. We gather as a group for High Days or weekly, monthly services or for rites of passages like weddings, births or deaths. The role or ritual is to share and celebrate our faith and our lives.

ADF has a prescribed format, a template that is followed for all High Day rituals referred to as the Core Order of Ritual, or COoR. Let's examine this in more detail.

ADF COoR (Core Order of Ritual)

As Established by the Clergy Council 2006

1. Initiating the Rite - May include:
   a. Musical Signal
   b. Opening Prayer
   c. Processional
   d. Establishing the Group Mind
2. Purification - This must take place prior to Opening the Gates
3. Honoring the Earth Mother
4. Statement of Purpose
5. (Re)Creating the Cosmos
   a. Sacred Center must be established in a triadic Cosmos
   b. The Three Worlds or Realms must be acknowledged
   c. The Fire must be included
   d. Sacred Center is most commonly represented as Fire, Well and Tree
6. Opening the Gate(s) - Must include a Gatekeeper
7. Inviting the Three Kindreds
8. Key Offerings - This will commonly include:
   a. Invitation of Beings of the Occasion
   b. Seasonal customs as appropriate
   c. Praise Offerings
9. Prayer of Sacrifice
10. Omen
11. Calling (asking) for the Blessings
12. Hallowing the Blessing
13. Affirmation of the Blessing
14. Workings (if any)
15. Thanking the Beings
16. Closing the Gate(s)

17. Thanking the Earth Mother
18. Closing the Rite

Initiating the Rite/Purification

Although ADF does not cast circles we do consecrate both time and space at the beginning of the ritual. This is done to separate the mundane from the spiritual. I have seen this done with a ringing of a bell, sounding of the horn, lighting of a candle or simply the priest raising his or her arms and announcing some opening phase. This helps create a sign post that we are entering sacred time. "All ritual, whether religious or not, should have a clearly designated beginning" (Bonewits, Neo Pagan Rites,25)

Once we have consecrated time we might need to consecrate ritual space. If we are using a Nemeton or land that has been set aside for religious/ spiritual purposes already, the need to consecrate the place might not be necessary. If we are using the public land such as parks or unmarked natural areas, then we will need to consecrate the site.

"Having begun the consecration of time, you need to immediately consecrate a bit of space. In a place that is normally used for religious activities, all you need to do is to walk into the temple or grove with a proper intent, and the sacred nature of the place will become activated. In a location that is normally mundane (or at least not normally viewed as sacred), you will need to mark the physical perimeter of the area you plan to use. This can be done loosely by processing around the area, or (if you are short on maneuvering room) by having everyone sit or stand in a circle (or other shape) and hold hands while singing a song about sacred space"

~Bonewits, "Step by Step through A Druid Worship Ceremony"

The space may be consecrated by smudging and asperging the site and all those who enter. I have also seen some groves sing songs or chants as they do this to further help the participants move from mundane to spiritual. The idea is "to help them [the participants] to focus on the events at hand by clearing away all irrelevant or incompatible thoughts" (Bonewits, Neo Pagan Rites, 26).

As previously stated, we don't cast circles, but we do define the outer boundary by opening the gates and creating a sacred or holy center. That sacred center is cut off from the mundane or chaotic world. Ceisiwr Serith says it best

"To be sacred is to be cut off. Most IE words used to describe sacred space derive from roots conveying the meaning "to cut" – templum, temenos, ve – the sacred is that which is cut off. Cut off from what? If a sacred space is to be a Cosmos, it must be cut off from Chaos. Not only is it ordered, but this order is defined in relation to disorder.

"Since the sacred cuts off, it is a border. It defines the difference between that which is inside and that which is outside. Borders must themselves be defined. They must be marked physically, established ritually, and reflect a mythical reality.

"The border (sacred), the center (holy), and the space between in which we perform our rites. Protected by the sacred border, blessed by the holy center, both we ourselves and the universe about us are brought into alignment. By ordering physical space to create sacred space, both microcosm and macrocosm are similarly ordered. We and the Cosmos are made perfect, complete and ordered"

~Serith, "The Place of Ritual"

Honoring the Earth Mother

The Earth Mother sustains us in ritual and in life. All that we have and all that we are is because of her gifts. In ritual, we open and close with her as both a way of grounding/centering and of helping create sacred space.

This offering becomes an internal cue for those who habitually attend ADF rituals that we are now separating ourselves from the mundane into the sacred. It serves as a reflective personal grounding and centering for me that continues to grow with our grove attunement. By repeating this step at the beginning and end of every ritual we are also creating and imprinting the signposts that help people settle into sacred space and then to return back to the mundane.

Statement of Purpose

This section of the ritual is pretty self-explanatory, why are you performing this ritual? Is it a seasonal ritual, a rite of passage, a full moon ritual? Whatever the reason, here is where you make the statement or pronouncement of intent.

(Re)Creating the Cosmos/Opening the Gates

ADF rituals start with a series of steps which help us transition from the mundane to the sacred and to establish a group mind, or group energy. Once these things are done and we are mentally and spiritually ready, we (re)create the sacred

Our goal here is to define the space around us and rearrange it such that the center of the worlds lies in our ritual space. We begin by acknowledging the three parts, or realms, of our world. There are several variations of the terminology that can be used to define the realms. Among the Celtic people, it was common to refer to the realms as The Land, The Sea and The Sky. Other variations are more generic, referring to them by location, such as Lower realm or Underworld, Middle realm and

Upper realm or Upperworld. Still further variations designate the Three Realms as well as the Three Worlds separately, and once the Three Gates are established, we see a sacred center created from nine holy things.

"The center of the world is a place where the deity(ies) created everything, and therefore the place that has access to everywhere. Selecting landmarks in the North, South, East and West from the center helps define reality, the territory that is known to your tribe. Sacred mountains, World Trees…all mark such a world originating point, and include the idea of a symbolic way to reach the other worlds"

~Bonewits, Neo Pagan Rites, 31.

So what about these Three Gates? The Gates are portals we plan to use to access these sacred places. In ADF rituals, our three gates are the Well, which leads to the Lower realm, the Fire, which leads to the Upper realm and the Tree, which leads to the Middle realm and bridges the gap between the lower and upper world to create one aligned center within our ritual space around which we have ordered the cosmos: our recreated cosmic space and sacred center

"In ritual, we do as the Gods did by re-creating the creation of Cosmos and of the universe. In so doing, we also re-create the time and place of that first creation. The Sacred Center is that place created in ritual where all the Worlds meet, and where a 'portal' can be opened, allowing communication between these cosmic planes. In this place, we can be in all Worlds at once and in all times at once. Here, anything is possible. In ADF worship, we do not seek to transport worshippers between the Worlds to celebrate our rites; rather we open a Gate between the Worlds"

~Our Own Druidry, 21

Once we have established the center, we are ready to transform the symbols of the Fire, Well and Tree to be those magical gates to all the worlds. We begin by "hallowing" or making holy/sacred each of the gates. Ian Corrigan has written a song, "The Portal Song," whose lyrics give ample instructions for hallowing the center. The Fire is blessed with poured oil, the Well is "silvered," meaning some form of silver is dropped into the water, and the Tree is often censed and aspersed with water from the well and incense or a smudge stick.

We call on a Gatekeeper to help us open the gates: The Fire as a portal to the Upper realm, The Well as a portal to the Lower realm, and The World Tree that stands firm in the center, a conduit between the worlds. I see the World Tree as the Celtic Tree with interlocking knot work that has the crown and roots woven together, reaching into all realms and thus connecting all realms together.

It is with help and magic of the Gatekeeper that we are able to open these gates. The Gatekeeper is usually a Deity and is oftentimes what is called a "psychopomp" meaning that he or she walks between worlds freely. As noted in many tales from lore of various cultures, it is not always easy to realm walk! My grove, Three Cranes Grove, has established a relationship with a Totem animal, Garanus Crane, as our Gatekeeper, and we have had great success.

We offer to the Gatekeeper and ask for his or her help to aid and ward us as we perform our ritual. "Once we have re-created the Center of the Worlds and consecrated the Hallows, we call upon a special, liminal God or Goddess to 'join their magic with ours' so that we might open those gateways to the

Three Worlds that have taken form in our Hallows. We call these deities Gatekeepers" (Our Own Druidry, 22).

With the gates open we will re-establish the center of the cosmos connecting all worlds, realms and times together in one sacred space. That allows us to send our thoughts, and praises to the Kindreds, offer sacrifices and to worship the kindred and in return we receive their blessings and wisdom. One metaphor for this whole process of defining a ritual center, or opening the gates, is that you are tuning the group mind's psychic awareness to whatever wavelength the ancestors, spirits and/or gods with be communicating on…"It doesn't matter whether you think you are creating the sacred center or merely recognizing or manifesting one that was already there" (Bonewits, Neo Pagan Rites, 33).

Understanding the Gates.

"In Our Druidic ritual we have come to build our ritual patterns around three key tools. The first, the ritual water, is kept in a vessel, often a cauldron, which we call the 'Well'. The second, live fire, is central to Pagan ritual. A metal vessel or tray holds the 'Fire', even if it is only a few candles and a holder for incense. The third key tool represents both the sacred center and the whole Order of the Worlds. A simple symbolic pillar or an image of a tall tree—just large enough to stand well above the Fire and Well—can serve as a ritual 'Tree.' This symbol has several cultural variations. Some might prefer an actual tree-shaped symbol, while others might prefer a tall stone, or a symbol of the World Mountain. In any case, these three symbols are commonly referred to as the 'Fire, Well and Tree'"

~Our Own Druidry, 49

Fire:

As stated above, the fire is the gate to the upper realm or heavens. It connects us to the Shining Ones.

Fire is sometimes connected to creativity, and it is through there that we call out to the powers of inspiration. Fire is the divine spark in all of us. It is the fire of order, it is the fire of transformation, it is the fire of sacrifice, and the fire of our hearth. Fire is called upon in the two powers meditation to mix with the waters of potential and to help balance and transform us. It connects us to the sky power. Fire is again called on to infuse the waters of life to create what Cei calls "fiery water."

Fire establishes a group or public hearth. Think about the bond that is established sitting around a fire. To feed the fire is to feed the Gods. Across all IE cultures fire is a common spiritual concept and tool.

Well:

The well is the gate to the lower realm or the Underworld. It connects us to our ancestors and the chthonic beings. "The Well is an ancient place of offering. The ancient Celts used to offer weapons, precious objects and even household goods to water" (Our Own Druidry, 22).

The well represents the underground waters the flow beneath us. It is these waters that we refer to in the two powers meditation; the waters of potential or chaos. It connects us to the Earth power. The well is also connected to memory, wisdom and wishing. Think about the wishing wells of folktales and our childhood. I think of the Norse myths regarding the well and of Odin sacrificing an eye for the wisdom of Mimir's Well. There is also the Well of Wyrd and the Well of Hvergelmir. (See everything ever written on Asatru' including Our Troth Volume 1.)

The well or water also represents rebirth and water as associated with our emotions. It is in the waters of life that we receive our blessings from the Well or Potential (Demissy, Sacred Space, an Exploration of the Triple Center).

Tree:

The tree is our axis mundi connecting all the worlds together as one. It also connects with the midrealm and the nature spirits. The tree gives us shelter, protection and food. It is the center of our sacred space.

"The Tree is the axis mundi or axis of the world. It is the cosmic pillar that holds up the sky and connects, through its roots, with the lands below our feet. Thus the Tree, while existing in the Midworld, connects all the Worlds above and below. It can be a tree, a mountain, an omphalos or even a pillar or boundary stone. But the Tree always stands at the center of our world"

~Our Own Druidry, 22

"Rooted deep and crowned high" is something that we say in ADF and I cannot think of a better visual, it's branches reaching high into the heavens and the roots digging far down into the underworld. Some examples of the World Tree could be Yggdrasil in the Norse myth or the Bile in Irish. In Roman or Vedic we could use Pillars as the axis mundi. For the Greeks, Mount Olympus served some of this purpose.

Inviting the Three Kindreds

The Three Kindred invocation (or invitation) is usually done after the Gates have been opened and is a way of asking the Kindred to join us for a few minutes, in sacred space. I feel the Kindred are always with us; listening and sending messages but this is a special invite to say please give us your attention. This is usually done through descriptive words, to help the entire attendants visualize the Kindred. Isaac Bonewits writes that the invocation has "two primary purposes: to invoke the attention of the god(s) and/or goddess(es) who are the focus of the rite, and to describe him/her/them to the worshippers clearly enough to enable everyone to get a psychic fix onto whom they will send their energy" (Bonewits, Neo Pagan Rites, 34).

I already reviewed the Three Kindred when we started daily devotionals so please review that section to refresh your memory.

Key Offerings/Prayer of Sacrifice

Once the gates have been opened and the cosmic/sacred center established then you could/would fill out the cosmic picture by telling a (cultural) story or myth etc to set the picture for the grove.

This would be the time to offer sacrifice(s) to the Deity(ies) of the occasion.

"Each of our rites is commonly dedicated to two or more of the Gods and Goddesses. These are usually chosen either for their connection with the seasonal holiday being celebrated, for their ability in the area of the work being done or their special relationship with the mortal focus of the rite. The Patrons of the rite are first invoked with expressive prose or poetry, sometimes accompanied by a visualized image of the Deities"

~Ian Corrigan, "The ADF Outline of Worship"

So to choose a focus for the Key Offerings then one must know why they are performing the ritual and be grounded in the lore enough to dress the ritual outline up for the occasion or Deity in which the offering is for.   If it is a high day then one could use the various myths surrounding that high day or use the lore to help set the seasonal motif.

If you were using a lunar cycle for new moons etc then you could borrow again from lore or corresponding monthly names and elements, example the Celtic names for the month and their meanings would lend itself to the offerings/Deities.

If you are doing protection rite or magical working then it comes to knowing what you need and knowing enough about the Deities and lore to do the work of the ritual.

Understanding the word sacrifice

Try as I might I don't think I can explain sacrifice any better than the quotes listed below. So in many cases I simply include the original quotes.

"In our time, the word 'sacrifice' has a negative connotation to some people, due to its use by the dominant religion to refer to its founder's agonizing death by execution. But the word comes from the Latin words sacer (sacred; to set apart) and facere (to make or to do). Thus its true meaning is "to make sacred, to set apart." And this is just what we do when we make our offerings to the Kindreds. And when we make these offerings, we are 'setting them apart' from the profane world, making them appropriate for the Kindreds"

~Our Own Druidry, 22

"This is the stage at which most ceremonies will have some form or another of "sacrifice". There's no room here to go into a general theory of sacrifice, so suffice it to say that the purpose of a sacrifice is to "feed" the Gods with as much psychic energy as possible, in order to trigger a return response of divine power"

~Bonewits, "Step by Step"

"This is the moment when every worshipper sends there love and respect, there energy, through the Gates to the Patrons and Powers"

~Ian Corrigan, "The ADF Outline of Worship"

"In an Indo-European Paleo-Pagan sacrifice, the gods were given small, usually inedible, parts of the animal. The rest was cooked and eaten by the people attending the rite. Some of the meat was thus transformed as a gift to the gods, born on the rising smoke of the fire. The rest was transformed into a gift from the gods – their divine fire transformed the animal into something sacred by cooking it"

~Ceisiwr Serith, "The Place of Ritual"

"At this stage all the energy, worship and aspiration of the participants is gathered up and offered in through the gate to the honored beings of the rite, along with a physical sacrifice. This is the hinge of the rite, after which the energy, which has been being directed into the gate, now turns and begins to flow back in turn"

~Our Own Druidry, 73

"So we offer sacrifice to the Kindred both as a way to build a relationship and as a form of honor and worship. First if we hope to establish a *ghosti relationship with the Kindreds then we must first offer up the gift, but even beyond that, if we hope to make that relationship personal and fulfilling, then we should follow the virtue of hospitality. We give out of love and respect, and having given, we ask what the Kindred give in return. Our

hope is that they will bless us with omens / blessings that will manifest in our lives. There is no guarantee that they will return the gift but having a healthy working relationship with the Kindreds is often times blessing enough. You get what you give, in sacrifices, ritual and life."

~*Our Own Druidy*, 22

"No wonder the first and apparently most obvious definition of "Piety" in Plato's Euthyphro, is "Sacrifice and prayer", which in turn means "to ask and to give," so that religion becomes a "craft or trade."

~Walter Burkert, *Creation of the Sacred*, 135

"Life is homoeostasis: a transient stability depending upon the "just" exchange; a precarious equilibrium in the flux of matter and energy"

~Burkert, *Creation of the Sacred*, 155

"So far I have really looked at reciprocity as a reason for sacrifice and this is probably the most often type of sacrifice we perform here in ADF, there are however other reasons for sacrifice. Sometimes we perform apotropaic offerings for averting evil or bad luck. Here, the sacrificer makes an offering to say, in effect, "Take this and go away", rather than forming a relationship with that power or deity. Outdweller Offerings could go in this type of offering/ sacrifice. "Gifts to the gods may be regarded as a tribute exacted by their threatening power"

~Burkert, *Creation of the Sacred*, 155

We also have the shared feast:

"The Shared Meal–Here we take food and eat some while giving the rest to the Kindreds. This act enhances the unity of the People through celebration, and allows communion with the Kindreds"

~*Our Own Druidry*, 23

"The central ritual of ancient sacrifice is sacred slaughter introducing the common feast"

~Burkert, *Creation of the Sacred*, 150

In these last two quotes, Kirk and Cei remind us that when "maintaining the Cosmic Order, when we give offerings that the unity of the people be enhanced, or the earth may be healed and strengthened, we are re-affirming the cosmic order," and "Chaos Mitigates Cosmos, too much order can cause brittleness. Think of a tree that cannot bend in the wind, and therefore breaks. In our rites, we have Praise Offerings, which cannot be totally controlled. Spontaneity in prayers, actions and praise can keep a ritual from becoming lifeless" (*Our Own Druidry*, 23).

I hope this helps people understand the importance of sacrifice in an ADF style druid ritual.

The Omen

Drum roll please. The Omen is the time we see if we did our job right, or at least good enough. We have given praise and honored the Kindreds and now we ask our questions...everyone waits with bated breath to see: have they been accepted? Most often they are, but there is that moment when the seer is pulling the omen and you being to run through the ritual in your mind, and yes, there are times when there is still work to do, more praise to be offered, unfinished business.

So what is the Omen? It is simply questions to the Kindred asking for guidance and blessings. Once we have given to them, what do they give us in return, if they choose to give something in return?

"One of the core skills of the Druid's art is divination—the use of magic to discover that which is unknown. We divine to determine what is unseen in the present and past, and what the pattern of Dan may hold for our future. In Druidic ritual we also often divine to determine whether the spirits are pleased with our work, whether our offerings have been accepted, whether our work is headed for a good outcome, and what kind of power is being offered by the spirits"

~*Our Own Druidry*, 44

"Success is achieved when one is ready to accept the sign at the appropriate moment, integrate it into the particular situation, and thus create or recreate a meaningful cosmos"

~Burkert, *Creation of the Sacred*, 159

The omen is explained in more detail in the next chapter.

The Blessings

The return flow is the hinge of the ritual. We establish the sacred center and fill out the cosmic picture, then we offer praise to all those Kindreds gathered. Once we have done that and given of ourselves, we ask for blessings. We take the omen and project it into the "waters of life," asking the grove to help manifest the omens into the waters, thus charging the waters with the blessings. The Kindreds give this blessings and council in the omen, but it is the distribution of the waters that symbolizes the acceptance of the blessings. Three Cranes most often will say something like "a gift for a gift, as we have given unto the powers so now we ask for a gift in return."

"The priest/ess invokes the Blessing as water drawn from the Well of Potentials and held in the light of the Fire of Transformation. We

contemplate again our needs and the Omen as we drink the Blessing. We often sing an anthem or listen quietly during this most reverent moment"

~Corrigan, *The ADF Outline*

Workings

Now that you have given to the Kindreds and have been blessed/filled with the return flow you are ready to do any workings in ritual space. This could include energy work, healing work, oaths etc…

Thanking the Beings

Pretty much just what you think, just as you invited the beings to the ritual you would now thank them for coming. This is done in reverse order with Diety(ies) of the occasion first, then the Kindreds.

Closing the Gates/Thanking the Earth Mother

You would now join your magic once again with the Gatekeeper and close the gates and to bookend the ritual and ground everyone back into the mundane world you would thank the Earth Mother. Many Groves when end with a chant/recessional.

I did save one optional segment of the COoR for last…

(Optional) The Outdwellers.

One of the most misunderstood and controversial parts of ADF rituals are the Out-dwellers offering and/or acknowledgement.

While on the surface, the offering itself may be to ask those powers whose purpose may be cross with ours to take this gift and leave us be for now. The questions begin to swirl once you start to dissect the "offering." Is it a sacrifice or offering? Is it a bribe? Are you establishing a *ghosti relationship with these beings? Should you be? Many among ADF now turn away during this part of the rite as to not establish a relationship with these powers of chaos and discord.

Some will offer a bottle only to kick it as they walk away. STOP...

All we are simply saying is that at this time and at this place there may be powers or beings that purposes or causes are different than ours and we ask them to leave us in peace to do our work. Not forever but for now.

Should we offer to them, yes and in my opinion we should at times welcome them into our lives and direct that energy for useful purposes.

The Out-dwellers serve their purpose throughout all Indo- European cultures, and I think it is fitting that we acknowledge them and respect them. An offering to them asking them to leave us be is more than appropriate and helps the members feel the shift in establishing sacred space. When the mind is free from worry, it is better able to disengage from reality as we know it and begin to feel the liminality of the space around us. It is also the time when we can let go of ill feelings in ourselves and enter into this ritual with an open heart and open mind. To me, it establishes a frith-stead for all.

I have seen and participated in rituals where a guardian has been called on to help protect the grove and I have mixed feelings about this. If you call the guardian before the Out-dwellers offering then are you assuming that the guardian will be unable to do the warding? It seems to me that you could argue that by calling a guardian after the Out-dwellers offering you are just adding insurance to the ritual in case the Out-dwellers break a "ghosti" relationship.

I for one don't see turning away from your potential enemy. First, it is dangerous, and second, it is disrespectful—as is kicking over the offering bottle or antagonizing them. These are powerful ancient beings, and we should hold a level of respect for them.

I would also add that as warriors, we are Out-dwellers living on the edges of society. Loved and feared, often at the same time, a good example of this would be the Manner bund.

The Warrior's Role in Group Ritual

What is the warrior's role in group ritual? The warrior's role should begin well before the ritual.

She should take complete inventory of emergency supplies available. Make sure there is water or a fire extinguisher in case of emergency.

Next she should evaluate the site. If indoors know all exits in case of a fire. If outdoors, locate cover or low laying area in case of storms or tornados.

She would also make sure there are no hazards in or around ritual site (broken glass, sharp corners, uneven steps etc). I would suggest that the warrior clean up the site. Picking up trash, cigarette butts etc. The warrior could then cleanse the site with sage and prayer, chant etc.

Being second function and having service as part of the warrior way, the warrior would also help carry and set up ritual.

The warrior and/or a healer could be one of the sensor / asperser at the beginning of the ritual since that could be considered cleaning and protection.

In many groves warriors have become the spiritual warder of the rite. I know at my grove a warrior almost always does the out-dwellers. In my mind this makes perfect sense; warriors are here to protect and serve the grove and what better way than ritually.

I think we need to evaluate the relationship we have with the out-dwellers and whether the warriors that do the out-dwellers offering should be allowed to do any other part in the ritual. Maybe they should stay out of the rite completely, disengaging and keeping an eye out for any issues. This would allow the warrior to be available to leave the ritual space to talk to anyone who showed up late, ensuring they are cleansed before entering the grove. Also if anyone was disrupting the rite or if the police or park ranger showed up in the middle of the rite, the warrior could meet with them and talk, hopefully while the rite continued. The role is not one of security but of warder, it is not about force but compromise.

I could also see the Warrior in the role of Warder be the one who opens in the gates and establishes the sacred center. Let me explain the magician that establishes the sacred center is the one responsible for "holding" those gates open with his/her magical partner (the gatekeeper) so the person should be holding/warding etc the entire time the gates are open hence the liturgical phases "join your magic to mine, aid and WARD us as we walk the elder ways..." the need to call a warder is redundant your warder is the gatekeeper...the person opening/holding/warding the sacred center is acting as a warrior/magician in this function so doing the "outdweller offering" could very well be a part of the magical service that the one in that role would perform.   There could be interesting liturgy written and added for this sacrifice that the warrior has made for the tribe.

That should just about give you a complete overview of an ADF ritual. Let's turn the page and look at Divination…

"The bravest are surely those who have the clearest vision of what is before them, glory and danger alike, and yet notwithstanding, go out to meet it. "

~Thucydides

Chapter 5

Warrior Divination

What is divination? To me divination is a way to talk to the Kindreds or to whatever power you believe is out there. Ask a question and seek an answer. You could look for omens in nature or talk to the Kindred(s) through divination. Skip Ellison writes "divination is a way of obtaining information. That information or knowledge can come from the Kindreds, from the subconscious mind of the person doing the divination or the unknown." (Ellison, The Solitary Druid 56)

Ian sums it up quite nicely, "divination is the use of magic to discover that which is unknown." I think it is important to acknowledge the fact that it is done through magic. It is also a skill that one must develop through practice and patience.

Ian also writes "In Druidic ritual we also often divine to determine whether the spirits are pleased with our work, whether our offerings have been accepted, whether our work is headed for a good outcome, and what kind of power is being offered by the spirits." It is the through the omens that we engage in the reciprocal relationship with the Kindreds, we have given to them through praise, offerings and/or sacrifice and now they in return give us blessings/advise through the omens.

There are many ways to divine. The most popular one used in Neo-Pagan circles today is sortilege.

Psychologist Julian Jaynes writes, "Sortilege (cleromancy)…consists of the casting of lots, or sortes, whether with sticks, stones, bones, beans, coins, or some other item. Modern playing cards and board games developed from this type of divination."

Here are some examples of IE cultures and their use of sortilege.

Germanic

A very popular method of divination used by today's neo-pagans is "pulling runes". The runic alphabet was first designed for writing. "The earliest inscription date from the late second century CE, but researchers are not sure how much earlier it was developed. Because most of the early writing was on wood, none of the early material has survived." (Ellison, The Solitary Druid 67)

Tacitus writes in Germania "For omens and the casting of lots they have the highest regard. Their procedure in casting lots is always the same. They cut off a branch of a nut bearing tree and slice it into strips; these they mark with different signs and throw them completely at random onto a white cloth." (Tacitus 10)

This is commonly believed to be an example of rune or pre-rune divination.

Celtic

Another popular method of divination among neo-pagans especially those on a Druid path is Oghams. Much like the runic alphabet it appears that the Ogham alphabet originated about the late second century CE. Skip writes that there are few references that Ogham was used as a divinatory tool but some people argue that Tacitus "may have been referring to Ogham rods as well as Rune staves." (Ellison, The Druids' Alphabet 2) In The Solitary Druid, Skip also reminds us of the tale "The wooing of Etain" where the druid Dalan "made three wands of yew, and upon the wands he wrote Ogham…" (Ellison, The Solitary Druid 62)

I also found the following information: "Wood was thought to have special properties for divination. In early Ireland one could learn the future by casting yew wands with ogham inscriptions upon the ground. In Fenian stories, wood shavings may help to find a missing or fugitive person." (answers.com)

So even if Oghams being used as a divination tool is a relatively new concept, I still think it is a valid method for the Modern Warrior to use. Again, I remind everyone that I'm a revisionist more than a Reconstructionist.

Greek

"Sortes Thriaecae, or Thriaen lots, were chiefly used in Greece; they were pebbles or counters distinguished by certain characters that were cast into an urn, and the first that came out was supposed to contain the right direction. This form of divination received its name from the Thriaej, three nymphs supposed to have nursed Apollo and to have invented this mode of predicting futurity.

Sortes Viales, or street and road lots, were used both in Greece and Rome. The person that wanted to learn his fortune carried with him a certain number of lots, distinguished by several characters or inscriptions. Walking to and fro in the public ways he asked the first boy whom he met to draw, and the inscription on the lot thus drawn was received as an infallible prophecy. Plutarch declared that this form of divination was derived from the Egyptians, by whom the actions and words of boys were carefully observed as containing in them something prophetical." (The Gale Group, Inc,)

Again, I'm not overly familiar with the Greeks but I do know that fellow ADF warriors use a type of divination sortilege that they have developed. It works and I see no reason why one cannot weave together scholarly information with UPG.

Since I follow a Norse path, I am currently using Runes as one of my divination methods. "The runic system may have well been fully developed by as early as 200 B.C.E. It is certain that the magico-religious practices of the ancient Germanic priesthood were aided by the use on many runic and/or pre-runic signs" (Thorsson 5).

I have been resistant to work with the Runes before but want to try to deepen my work and understanding of this system. I think that some of my resistance is that so many people use them and have such a good understanding of them that I feel that I have nothing to add.

For the work that I am currently doing I am pulling either one rune as an omen to reflect on, asking each of the Kindreds for their input, or drawing three Runes, one from each Kindred.

Here is a very quick review of the Runes and some very basic keywords to get you started:

The Runic Symbols

Rune	Name	Translation(s); Meaning(s)
ᚠ	Fehu	**Cattle;** movable wealth, generosity
ᚢ	Uruz	**Auroch, drizzle;** strength, dross
ᚦ	Þurisaz	**Giant, thorn;** chaotic, brute strength
ᚨ	Ansuz	**Mouth, god;** beginnings, communication
ᚱ	Raiðo	**Journey;** horse-and-rider, partnership
ᚲ	Kenaz	**Torch, ulcer;** cheer, pain, death
ᚷ	Gebo	**Gift;** reciprocity, *ghos-ti-*
ᚹ	Wunjo	**Joy;** bliss
ᚺ	Hagalaz	**Hail;** destruction, challenge
ᚾ	Nauðiz	**Need;** oppression, lessons learned
ᛁ	Isa	**Ice;** beautiful and dangerous
ᛃ	Jera	**Year;** good harvest, hard work
ᛇ	Eihwaz	**Yew;** ancient lore, helping and hurting
ᛈ	Perþo	**Dice cup, vulva;** joy, uncertainty
ᛉ	Algiz	**Elk-sedge;** offensive/defensive balance
ᛊ	Sowilo	**Sun;** warmth, strength, promise, cycles
ᛏ	Tiwaz	**Tir;** guidance, justice, navigation
ᛒ	Berkano	**Birch;** strength, flexibility, resourcefulness
ᛖ	Ehwaz	**Horse;** easy and joyful travel, help

ᛗ	Mannaz	**Man;** self, mortality, *orlog*, kinship
ᛚ	Laguz	**Water;** change, hidden wealth, flowing
◇	Ingwaz	**Ing;** fertility, ancestors
ᛞ	Dagaz	**Day;** rising sun, new day, deliverance
ᛟ	Oþila	**Enclosure;** stationary wealth, ancestors, completion

The Ogham Symbols

Few	Name	Tree	Meaning(s)
├	Beith	**Birch**	New beginnings, purification
├	Luis	**Rowan**	Beauty and delight, magical protection
├	Fern	**Alder**	Protection, guidance
├	Sail	**Willow**	Liminality, flow
├	Nion	**Ash**	Weaver's beam, connection
┤	Uath	**Hawthorn**	Fear, despair, cleansing
┤	Dair	**Oak**	Strength, knowledge
┤	Tinne	**Holly**	Balance, mastery
┤	Coll	**Hazel**	Wisdom
┤	Ceirt	**Apple**	The Otherworld, shelter, choice
┼	Muin	**Vine**	Challenge, communication, inspiration
┼	Gort	**Ivy**	Growth, pathways
┼	nGéadal	**Broom**	Healing and tools
┼	Straif	**Blackthorn**	Secrets, strife, transformation
┼	Ruis	**Elder**	Passion, embarrassment, endings
┼	Ailm	**Silver Fir**	Foresight, inception, perspective

⊥	Onn	**Gorse**	Easy travel, wheel, movement
≣	Úr	**Heather**	Earth and growth, death
≡	Eadhadh	**Aspen**	Grief and fear, vision, communication
≣	Iodhadh	**Yew**	Ancestors and death, memory
✳	Éabhadh	**Poplar**	Buoyancy and healing, rising up
◇	Ór	**Spindle**	Work, building, wealth, domesticity
℅	Uillean	**Honeysuckle**	Drawing together, sweetness
⋈	Phagos	**Beech**	Ancestral knowledge
⊞	Emancholl	**Witchhazel**	Magic, illness/healing

TIP 1: If you do not own your own symbol set, you can draw the symbols on index cards for a quick, makeshift rune or ogham deck. Alternatively, you can purchase some craft wood at your local craft store and draw the symbols on with a permanent marker.

TIP 2: On ogham tiles, put a small inverted "v" on the bottom of the line that runs down the middle. Having the ^ at the bottom of the few will help you determine which end is "up." Runes are unique enough not to require directional assistance.

As you saw in the chapter on Daily devotions, you could pull a rune with your daily ritual, to make it more "warrior" I have done a few different types of lot casting. Here are a couple of examples.

I pull three runes; one for lessons of the mind, one for lessons of the heart or spirit and one for the lessons of the body. This continues the motif of the Warrior Triad.

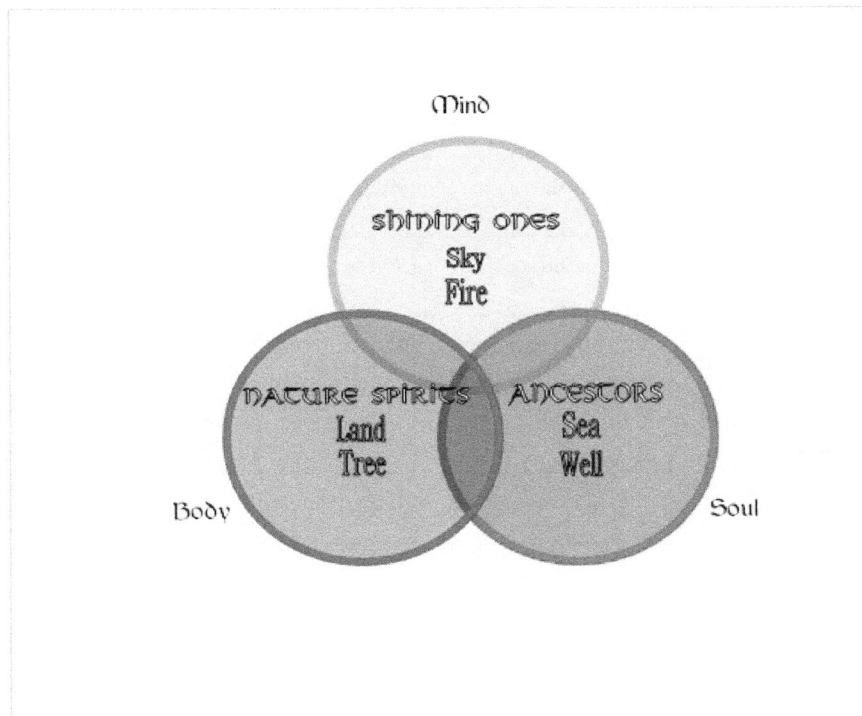

Mind

shining ones
Sky
Fire

NATURE SPIRITS
Land
Tree

ANCESTORS
Sea
Well

Body

Soul

So I pull runes something like this at the end of my daily/weekly ritual.

"A gift for a gift, I have offered you praise and offerings.

Now I ask of you, mighty ones, Ancestors what lessons of the spirit do you offer to me to reflect upon?"

(pull rune)

"Noble ones, Nature Spirits what lessons of the body do you have for me to reflect upon?"

(pull rune)

"And Now Shining Ones, Our mother's first children, what lessons of the mind do you have for me to reflect upon?"

(pull rune)

Another way to work with warrior divination would be to assign certain deities to certain days and do daily praise offerings to them and pull an omen from them. I have a mixed pantheon an choose certain deities on certain days because it works for me. My wife does Norse in the morning and Celtic in the evening.

- Sunday – Belanus
- Monday - Angus Mac'Og
- Tuesday – Tyr
- Wednesday – Odin
- Thursday – Thor
- Friday – Garanus
- Saturday - Bridgit

As you can see some of them are not warrior deities but they are my matron and patron posse. My own UPG went into the order of which deity for which day. Belanus is a Gaulish" solar deity of my grove works with. Angus was the first that I called to so many years ago. Tyr, Odin and Thor are my offence line, with Tyr being the first to seek me out. Garanus is also Gaulish and means "with cranes" but my grove has used it as a proper name or title to the Crane that guides our grove. Lastly but certainly not least Lady Brighe, she tapped me on the shoulder and helps me remember my creative side. You however could choice all warrior deities; you can use a mix of Kindreds. Again the choice is yours.

I also have been known to do Native American stuff on a lunar cycle. When I do this I tend to work with my animal allies. (more of this later.)

As is the truth with many things so much of this divination is about doing.. A word of caution about rune sets and books, there is NO blank rune. It should be kept as a back up only. If a book has any hogwash about the blank rune put the book back on the shelf and keep looking for a book by Paxon or Thorsson.

Of course this is just an example using Runes, you just as easily use Oghams, tarot cards and quite often I use my Animal Medicine Cards. If you do decide to work with Ogham, I suggest picking up the book Skip Ellison's book "The Druids Alphabet" to help you begin your work with them.

Assignment 5

Begin to take an omen as part of your devotionals. Add this information to your journal entries. Reflect on how the omen affects your life, if it does? Are you gaining insights into your life? Are there reoccurring omens or patterns?

"Things do not change; we change".

~Henry David Thoreau

Chapter Six

Warrior Magic

As we explore the notion of warrior magic, consider it broken down into five parts:

1. Energy Work
2. Grounding
3. Animal Allies
4. Protection/Warding
5. Consecrating Tools

Part 1 – Energy Work

What do you see when you look in the mirror? Who is that staring back at you? Is it a mild manner man or woman or is there something more in those eyes? Many of us know there is something there, some energy that we can tap into for strength, for anger, for passion. Most of my generation grew up lying on the floor every Friday night looking at big Lou painted green and growling. We have all felt that energy in the heat of an argument or while driving on the interstate. That primal warrior energy, that many spend a lifetime trying to control or suppress.

What this chapter hopes to do is explore and harness that energy. To be a warrior is learning to control oneself. Don't ignore that energy and those feelings but learn to put them to use for you. How many of us have kept those passionate feelings bottled up only to pop a cork later or worse, they manifest themselves as other health issues. It's ok to be angry, passionate, emotional, and aggressive in the right context and focused in the right direction.

I have a saying "good things happen when you're aggressive." I don't mean argumentative or rude. I mean confident, sure of yourself. Not afraid to live life. Have you ever heard about a sports team playing on their heels? Or watch a football team blow a game playing prevent defense? There is a saying about how a good defense is a good offense and it's true: you can't win if you don't attack. Again, I'm are not talking about being rude or engaging in inappropriate behavior, I'm talking about living life to the fullest. There is another old saying about just this: it is better to live one day as a lion than a thousand as a lamb. Be aggressive in planning your goals and working toward achieving them. Don't be a by-stander in life. Always be working toward a goal, toward bettering yourself. Be active always; if you're not moving ahead you are moving backwards. To the victor go the spoils! So if you walk the warrior path; walk lively.

Tapping into that energy is something that we started earlier in our work. The daily or weekly meditations are the basic exercises that you will now begin to build on for energy work.

Energy Exercise One

Items you may want to use
1. Drumming CD
2. Incense
3. Candle

Start the CD (if you want) and light the incense. Do devotional prayer and use the meditation technique that you learned earlier in the book.

Once you are ready, begin taking slightly deeper than normal breaths...

In and out...look into the flame of the candle, focusing your energy there. See the flame as it flickers and burns.

Focus on making the candle burn brighter, breathing deeper and steady. In your mind's eye see the flame of your heart shrine burning. Feel the two flames reaching out and joining together.

Burning bright, feeding each other energy. See and feel the energy building in your chest, warm and healthy. Flowing from your heart shrine down your legs and arms, flowing up and crowning around your head. So that the flame of the candle and the fire or your heart shrine is flowing through you, feel the heat warm your bones, feel the heat burn away all negativity.

Feel the flames burning and coursing through you, awakening every fiber of your being.

Embrace the energy and allow it to wash over you, take what you need and allow it to start to die down, slowing retreating back up your legs, your arms back, back slowly to where it is once again just a small coal bed in your heart shrine awaiting the next time you need this energy...once again you see the candle in front you, just a flame...relax, stretch and feel the energy still lingering in your body, take this energy with you throughout the day or sit and ground and allow it fade away like the dying sunset.

Energy Exercise Two

Items you may want to use
1. Drumming CD
2. Incense

Start the CD (if you want)and light the incense. Do devotional prayer and use your meditation technique

Once you are ready begin taking slightly deeper than normal breaths…

In and out…as you breathe in and out use your hands and with every in breath bring your hands into your chest and with every out breath push your hands outward, palms away, fully extended.

Continue this in slow even breaths and feel the energy build around, feel the energy begin to crackle, and the hair on the back of your neck stand. When you feel you have built some energy then in your mind's eye turn to the coal bed of your heart shrine and see those coals once again begin to burn bright.

See and feel the energy building in your chest, warm and healthy. Allow the flames to extend down your arms, following the in and out movements that you make with each breath.

Allow the energy to pool around your hands, making an energy ball that engulfs your hands. Now begin to extend that ball away from your hands, like a yoyo the ball moves out and in, out and in.

Play with this energy and when you are ready stop, and then hold you're your hands out, palms up and let then energy once again begin to pool there, with every in breath pull the energy back into you, slowing collecting the energy, back, back into your heart shrine until there is again just a small coal bed in your heart shrine awaiting the next time you need this energy… relax, stretch and feel the energy still lingering in your body, take this energy with you throughout the day or sit and ground and allow it fade away like the dying sunset.

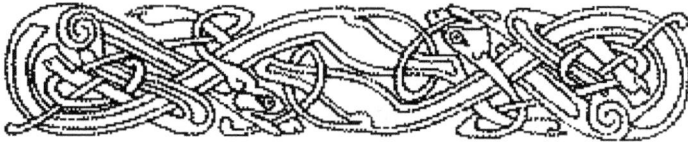

As you do this exercise you can begin to do more with the energy ball. You can allow it to grow into a bigger ball; it can encircle you and be used as a protective shield. It can be used to build healing energy that is focused to the one who needs healing. It can be used for warding and protecting people and places.

As a warrior for ADF, I am often called upon to perform the "out-dweller" portion of the ritual, and using this simple energy building technique to encircle myself before facing the "out-dwellers" has been very useful.

I have used exercise one when I was feeling drained or tired and really drew/built the energy to charge myself with an "energy shot," better than any over the counter energy drink! I also think it is very useful to burn away self-doubt and negativity.

Here is an example of how to do the energy work in a group setting:

Group Energy Exercise

Once you are ready begin taking slightly deeper than normal breaths…in and out…

As you breathe in and out, use your hands and with every in breath bring your hands into your chest and with every out breath push your hands outward, palms away, fully extended.

Continue this in slow even breaths and feel the energy build around, feel the energy begin to crackle, and the hair on the back of your neck stand.

When you feel you have built some energy then in your mind's eye turn to the coal bed of your heart shrine and see those coals once again begin to burn bright.

See and feel the energy building in your chest, warm and healthy.

Allow the flames to extend down your arms, following with the in and out movements that you make with each breath.

Allow the energy to pool around your hands, making an energy ball that engulfs your hands.

Now begin to extend that ball away from your hands, like a yoyo the ball moves out and in, out and in.

Take note of what color this energy is? See it flowing about you. Rising up and crowning about your head and flowing like a waterfall down your face and arms…down your chest and legs.

Feel this energy as it courses through you. This is your energy called upon to burn away all that is bad; called upon to be your physic shield. Feel it pulsing with your heartbeat creating an aura around you bright and vibrant.

Take a moment and just be in this space, in this energy.

In your mind's eye open up yourself to the others in the room and see their energy. Reach out and grab hold of the hands of those around you and feel your energy blend and mix with theirs. Feel their energy now rising up your arms and flowing through you to the next person until we are flowing together like a conduit of electric energy. See the energy of the group, vibrant, electric, orange, as it flows around the room, creating a wall, creating a ball that shields us all, flowing and pulsating. Growing brighter and stronger as we add our energy to the group…

Take a deep breath and enjoy the energy we have created. Now with everyone focused, think to yourself who needs this energy. Friends or family that needs healing? Picture those people in your mind's eye and send this energy out to them…if you have no one in your mind simply focus of lending your energy to those here who are sending it out…here in the sacred center…is the gate…send it thru the candle out and to them to the fires of their heart shrine.

Now let go of those around you and hold your palms up and let then energy once again begin to pool there, with every in breath pull the energy back into you, slowing collecting the energy, back, back into your heart shrine.

Feel the energies of those gathered here separate and flow back…becoming single colors…back, back up your arms, your legs…drawing back…back to your center…

Until there is again just a small coal bed in your heart shrine awaiting the next time you need this energy… relax, stretch and feel the energy still lingering in your body, take this energy with you throughout the day or sit and ground and allow it fade away like the dying sunset.

At this point you're probably thinking, well this is all well and good, but what does this have to do with controlling your emotions and your opening statement? How about everything: meditation, exercise and energy focus has a lot to do with your general outlook and how you deal with everyday stresses. Read on Grasshopper...

Part 2 - Grounding

Sometimes it's about calming down or grounding oneself. We have all had those days when we just had chaotic energy. Frantic, short fused...well here is a grounding exercise for you to try.

Take a deep breath, filling your lungs with a slow an easy breathe, hold it and slowly exhale counting slowing to yourself.

Try to count to nine, and hold for three count and then out for nine. As you do this try to relax your head and neck, roll your head slowly letting the tension release its hold on you.

Shake your arms and allow yourself to settle into yourself. Breathing deep and easy, in your mind's eye see a meadow in the summertime...

Feel the soft breeze on your skin. Feel the summer sun shining down to warm your face. Hear the sounds of summer, the birds, the wind in the trees, the sound of insects buzzing around you.

See yourself lay down in the grass, smell the sweet smells of honeysuckle and summer in your nose. Breathe deep and feel your weight even on the ground. Feel the embrace of your Mother Earth as she holds you in her bosom. Listen closely and hear her heart beat...

Slow and steady. Relax and allow yourself to match her rhythm. Feel her coolness as it seeps into your back relaxing you, calming you.

Feel again the warmth of Father Sun comforting you, feel these two powers of earth and sky mingle in you, relaxing you, caressing you. Know that you are loved. When you are ready breathe deep again and bring yourself back, back to the here and now bring with you that love. Feeling calm and relaxed open your eyes and go about your day.

There is still more! Working with your ancestors and animal allies will also help you access and direct warrior energy:

Part 3 - Animal Allies

Many of us who walk an Earth based religious path have worked with totem animals before, and if you already have a relationship with one, then I would suggest you continue to work with that animal. You may want to review that animal and ask what "warrior aspect" you can learn from it. Below is a ritual that you can perform that may help you to find your ally. Others chose to seek their totem through real life encounters and sightings so you must be attuned to what is going on around you. Do you see more red tail hawks in your travels than ever before?

Do you point them out to others who rarely see them? Maybe you should begin a relationship with that animal, again modifying the ritual listed in the book.

I picked my totems using an animal tarot deck many years ago. Before I joined ADF, and very early on my path I picked the blue heron and deer/stag. Not very warrior like but as I come to find out they are perfect for me. I later joined Three Cranes Grove and the crane/heron totem has become a very powerful, wonderful guide—a few years after I picked these totems.

I was at a festival here in Ohio and decided to go for a hike. As I wandered down and around a creek bed I turned and came face to face with a big buck. I must have been barely two feet away from him. I looked at his 8 or 10 point antlers, I smelled his musky scent and swallowed hard and froze. All I was thinking was up this close, one swing of his head and I would be gutted. He stared at me, well really glared at me as if to say, "Not quite like Bambi am I, big boy?" Then he snorted at me with disgust and leapt away. After that encounter I begin to research deer, stag and hart, and really began to work with that ally. It was later that I started Sacred Hart Warrior Lodge in honor of the energy of the stag. There are lessons to be learned from every animal, tree and rock if we open ourselves to their instruction.

Another aspect we must remember when talking about warrior animal allies is it was during the hunter/gatherer time period that warrior magic began. It was the traits of a good hunter that become the beginnings of the archetypes of the warrior and the magician.

As the hunter became more attuned to the animal that he hunted, the more successful the hunt was, and the hunter that could predict and lead the hunting party on successful hunts became more revered and powerful himself. It is from these roots we see totem magic begin. As the hunter/Wiseman began to understand the animal's patterns of eating, mating, drinking habits, etc, then he was better able to read the animal's scat and tracks. This became the tribe's first Wiseman/shaman.

Make sure you take the time to learn about your animal ally. Go to the park or zoo and sit, watch and learn. Here is a meditation / journey to help you find your nature (or other) ally.

Nature Ally Meditation

Close your eyes and prepare yourself for a journey.

Breathe deep and exhale slowly. In and out, slow and steady. Feel you body relax.

Feel the tension of the day fade away…rising like steam off your body or draining down your legs and out of your body.

Relax and when you are ready see in your mind's eye a path before you. This is a path that wanders through the woods before you. Follow the path into the trees. See the trees and growing green things all around you. Smell the earth on the wind. See the sunlight as it dances with the shadows down through the canopy of the trees.

See now up ahead of you a clearing. See a campsite and a welcoming fire. Go to the fire and look around. Find a place and sit and relax by the fire. See the flames of the fire as they lick and dance across the wood. Sit there and learn to be still.

Just be.

Hear the sounds of the forest. What do you hear? DO you hear the sound of a bubbling creek or waves lapping at a distant shore? Do you hear birds calling out their messages of life? Just sit and take in the world around you and when you are ready call out "I am ready, I come here seeking aid, seeking an ally. I am a warrior and I seek the guidance of the Kindreds. What lessons do I need to learn? What totem, ancestor or deity should I look to as a guide?"

Then wait, watch and listen to see what comes to you.

Do not get discouraged if nothing does simply enjoy the setting and be aware...

If someone or thing does step forward then begin to communicate with them. Begin the first steps to building that relationship. When you are done bid them farewell and begin your journey home.

Back the way you came. Back through the woods, back on the path....relax and remember your journey. When you are ready open your eyes and find yourself back, back to where you began.

Assignment 6

Write down in your journal what happened. If you made a connection, write down what was said, what you felt, what you learned. Research what you found. If it was an animal ally, I might suggest you look up information on that animal to find out what lessons they teach you. A good book for this is *Animal Spirits* by Ted Andrews. Pay attention to the warrior aspect of the guide. If you made a connection, then I would suggest that you do a weekly journey to sit with your guide and talk, learn and build a kinship with them. If you didn't then continue to try, and remember the old saying, when the student is ready, the teacher will appear."

Part 4 - Protection/Warding

There are many ways one could go about warding themselves. Ian Corrigan has a wonderful prayer called "The Armoring" that you can find in his book Sacred Fire, Holy Well. I do something similar but not as long but that I do as part of my Outdwellers offering:

Outdwelles Offering:

Spirits of Land I call on you this day and ask that you that you aid and help me to stand firm.

Spirits of Sea I call on you this day and ask that you that you aid and help me to stand proud.

Spirits of Sky I call on you this day and ask that you that you aid and help me to stand tall.

Now filled with the powers of land, sea, and sky I am aided, warded and protected and stand ready as a warrior for this grove.

Outdwellers, Outdwellers, I call out to you this day, not in friendship, nor in warning but in simple acknowledgement. You who stand against us, whose purpose may be cross with ours. I as a warrior of this grove sacrifice myself for the good of all and give you ghosti. A give for a gift, keep this old bargain.

Outdwellers and leave us be.

May there be peace in the East, in the south, to the west and to the north, above and below.

Likewise good people – as we gather here let all ill will, doubt, stress and fear leave your body and dissipate on the wind. Enter now will an open heart and open mind. May there be peace among us.

• • • • •

I also carry a "medicine bag" that has special items in it like tokens, gems, and herbs. I would suggest that you become familiar with the special properties that gems, crystals and herbs have so that you can use them as warrior tools. I have also made and used herb bags that I can carry, hang on car windows or place under a pillow. I used herbs like Mullein Leaf, Nutmeg, and/or crystals like Amber, Goldstone and Quartz to name a few.

This past year at the Earth Warriors Festival I had a chance to sit and talk with Alaric Albertsson after his workshop on Rune work and how to use them for protection. He has a great way of making bindrunes, a single symbol that represents and carries the magic of a selected set of runes, that one could either make in the air in front of them using a knife or their hand or that can be written on paper and carried in your pocket or glove box. Take two or three Runes and put them together to make your bind Rune, for example let's put Tiwaz with Auroch and Thurisaz. You would simply layer them one over the other until they make a bindrune. It would something like this:

There is also the act of walking through your house or the perimeter or your property with fire and saying a chant to Thor or another Deity for protection. We have a chant in ADF that we sometimes use "By the Light of the fire and might of the waters, this grove is made whole and holy." I'm sure that could be adapted. There is also a hallowing using a hammer, or walking the land with sage. I have also seen protection symbols places above the door and at windows. We have a Thor's stone by the front door in the garden and a Brigit's Cross over our front door. So there are many options for you to explore.

Part 5 – Consecrating Tools

As you begin to walk your warrior path you will begin to pick up tools that you use in your work. A medicine bag, athame, sword, herbs, crystals etc…it is important to consecrate these items and make them sacred. What I do is perform a regular ritual and then after the omen I use the blessings to consecrate the items. I say something like with this:

Consecration Prayer

With the flames of my piety I ask the Kindreds to bless this _____.

With the fire of my devotion I consecrate this tool to be used in my work. May the Kindreds bless this tool and all my work.

[Smudge the item with sage or incense lit from the candle]

From the well of rebirth and the cup of magic I call again on the might of the Kindreds bless cleanse and empower this _____.

[Sprinkle water from the well on the item]

Now with the powers of fire and water joining together, I ask the Kindred to hear my prayer and make sacred this tool.

• • • • •

This is just the beginning of what we can do once we tap into the magic of the warrior. Other warrior magic/rituals that we can return to would be sweat lodges, vision quest and rites of passages. We have become disconnected with the ebb and flow of our lives and the road signs that rites of passage help celebrate. Here is an example of initiatory test/rites of passage as described in the Book of Troth: "In several Indo-European cultures there were two different milestones in a young man's life. The first came when he took up arms and was initiated in the band of young warriors living on the margins of tribal society (Mannerbund) at about the age of fourteen. The second was when he gained property, married and became a full member of the tribe." (K.H.Gundarsson 248) Further examples of these rites of passage might include the wilderness passage where the basic paradigm is the subject withdraws from society and goes into the wilderness to live with an all male group for a time.

Again, another is the soul passing outside the realm of humanity. (Shape shifting into bear, wolf, etc) There is also total separation and a fight for life (subject would encounter near death or symbolic death and rebirth). We see this many times in legends and myths. Lastly, another popular rite of passage was the slaying of the monster, this often times had the eating of the dragon or lions heart etc so that the subject would take on wisdom, strength, etc of the slain monster.

So we have the basis for work that we can use to develop a system for warrior magic that would serve us in today world.

We see athletes psych themselves up before a match or game—perhaps this is the same energy that created the berserkers. Many of you have read or heard about the mind/muscle connection or other types of visualization techniques; this is just a watered down version of the warrior energy that we can tap into. It is here that we begin to apply what was with what is to be. Every journey begins with the first step. As in all things in this book it is up to you to walk your path and develop systems and routines that help you increase your warrior magic. These are just samples to get you started, but the work is yours to do...so get started.

"We must learn not to disassociate the airy flower from the earthy root, for the flower that is cut off from its root fades, and its seeds are barren, whereas the root, secure in mother earth, can produce flower after flower and bring their fruit to maturity. "

~Kabbalah

Chapter Six

Earth Warrior

What does it mean to be an earth warrior? As I have stated elsewhere in the book, we as warriors must be the stewards of the land. We must be the guardians of our Mother Earth. In principle, this may be a high idea, but in practice, it is self preserving. We must look at the impact we are making in the world around us; if not for us, then for the next generation.

I'm not one of the pagans that like to go around "Christian Bashing," but I do think that the prevailing western "Christian" thought process that considers the earth as temporary and something for "Man" to have dominion over has done nothing good for our situation. Having said that, I think we also do ourselves a disservice by believing that the Paleopagans were much different than us.

IE Cultures/Natural Resources

"Throughout most of Europe beginning roughly about 600 BC recycling service was on Tuesdays unless it fell on a high day then it would fall to the next day. This became a real problem for Rome as they begin to celebrate more and more holidays..." OK, I'm sorry but I get really tired of the myth of the noble savage. Make no mistake, regardless of what culture, the land and its resources were there for the taking.

The Indo-Europeans did not have the concept of exhaustible resources. The Vikings would cut down tree after tree to make their longboats (mainly this happened in Iceland). The popular Irish myth of Lugh and his step-mother Tailtiu could be an allegory for how the land died after being cleared for settlement. Migration seems to be the clear choice for overcrowding or depletion of local resources.

Indo-European cultures had economies based on stockbreeding, agriculture, hunting and fishing, so they connected to nature in way that may be hard for us in an urban setting to understand and relate to. Most of the modern world buys meat already butchered and wrapped. We are far removed to the life force of the food we eat. To kill something and know that it was alive at a very personal level is something that few of us have ever had to deal with, so from that perspective, they had a closer relationship to nature than we do (Fields, The Code of the Warrior, 16).

From the hunter gatherer nomadic lifestyles to the settled agricultural communities, their awareness of nature and understanding of its rhythms were much greater than ours. Their understanding of nature's patterns and how those patterns affect crops, herds, and prey was much more attuned than ours. There is proof that Proto-Indo-Europeans understood and had words for the by-products of domestic animals. There are words for dairy products, yokes, and wool so they did understand the resources these animals provided for them (Mallory, In Search of the Indo-Europeans, 126).

So their awareness and closeness to nature was much more attuned to the spirits around them, but their understanding of resources where not much different than ours and the last several generations. It is only in the last 75 to 100 years that we have been faced with the knowledge of limited resources. I know there was a basic scientific knowledge before that but I mean in the general public forum. When we settled America we did so with the same abandonment that our ancestors settled Europe. We now see the same industrial revolution in South America, and they, too, continue the wholesale clearing of land. On whole scale, we still don't truly understand the concept of limited resources.

So what can we do? What should we do? I for one am a member of the Sierra Club and Earth Warriors. I support Greenpeace, and there are many things great and small that we can do everyday.

The most obvious thing is Recycling. Our house is one of only three in our neighborhood that recycles (or at least has curb-side recycling, many say they take them to the area bins). I am saddened and amazed by the amount of waste that I see in the overflowing neighborhood trash bins. What I have noticed is that we can go two or three weeks without taking the trash can to the curb. This is very painful the week after Christmas when I see the amount of trash going to the landfill. The mountains of trash that we leave behind and the lasting effects on Mother Earth and all her children just sicken me.

I get really angry when I see pagans throwing away items without recycling. I hate to hear the excuses that it's just not convenient to recycle at festivals. So who cares if it convenient on not? It's certainly more convenient than finding a new world to live on! Talk about walking the walk.

I next item would be the community cleanup work that our grove does. We have adopted a park or park trail and we have even done work in a local cemetery. It is a great time when the grove gets together for this. There is something about working together that builds community. It is a time of work and conversation and it really brings us closer, almost as though community bonding is a gift we are given in return for stewarding the land.

Other things that make a difference is my wife is vegetarian, and although I eat meat I do try to limit the amount of red meat due to the damage that cattle are doing on the earth. Not just the methane gasses but the amount of water and feed needed to maintain the livestock is not good on the environment

We also just started a compost bin, and we have plans to install a rain barrel next year. We looked into solar panels for our house but we just can't afford it at this time. So regardless of what you do – do something. Be active in your community. Look up information about your local watershed. Find out about recycling and other ways to lesson your footprint. Also, read your local papers and different sites on the internet to research local companies and their practices. Find out who is the worst pollution offenders and find out what you can do. There are many citizen action groups and national groups available and need your help. Also just be aware, plant local nature plants in your yard, don't use birdseed as offerings (they germinate), don't use paper plates at rituals and gatherings.

The Promise

Here is a story from a long time ago. It is a story my grandfather used to tell me when I was curled up on the couch between him and my grandmother. He would often times tell me stories and he would had such a great sense of timing. He understood the use of silence. He taught me many things in these stories. He would say to me listen with your heart and I will tell you a story… and so he would begin.

Momma, I'm scared.

I know little one.

What will I eat?

Sister Rabbit will feed you.

What will I wear?

Brother Deer and Bear with clothe you.

What if I'm cold?

Bother Oak and Sister Willow will burn bright for you.

Will I be alone Momma?

No my child, your brothers and sisters are everywhere. Listen to the wind sing through the trees, the laughter of the bubbling brook, in all my creatures there is a voice my child, listen with your heart not your ears…if you are lonely just look into the nighttime sky, and you will see Grandmother Moon smiling down on you, gaze onward and see your ancestors in the stars.

But Mamma…

No more buts little one, it is time for sleep, curl up into my bosom and let me warm you through the night. Someday you will grow to be the mightiest of all my children, and your children and their children. You must promise me that you will listen with your heart and help care for your brothers and sisters. They can teach you much but you must remember what they say. Teach your children the lessons of the forest and of the meadows. Teach them to love your Mother and all things big and small...

I will Momma, I promise....

Assignment7

Research your local nature. Go to a local park and perform a quite ritual between you and the nature spirits. Walk through the park or woods around your house. Write in your journal your reflections.

Assigment 8

Research your local watershed and find the major sources of air and water pollution in your area, what the biggest source of pollution in your area is, and what impact it has.

"I am always doing that which I cannot do, in order that I may learn how to do it."

~Pablo Picasso

Chapter Seven

Lessons learned?

So as you have read through this book I hope that you have started to develop an idea or understanding of what being a warrior in the world today means to you. The basic idea is to capture the essence of the warrior and layer that energy into your life. Regardless of your spiritual path, family, health, job or education the warrior inside you awaits. How you embrace that warrior and allow it to manifest in your life is a truly personal experience. What I have tried to do is lay out some ideas to help you explore the warrior path on your own. This is not a path on which everything is handed to you. It is a path that you must engage in. For me it is an ever changing path of self-discovery and improvement, of challenges, defeats and victories. But with each step I have learned the real lesson…the lesson of me. I encourage you to do the same. Discover yourself.

For most of my work I focus on the hunter/gatherer time period in history. It is here that I feel the essence of the warrior spirit begins and where we can easily tap back into the warrior energy or archetype

Once we left the tribal paradigm and entered into the citizen soldier and later paid military personnel, some of the true essence of the warrior archetype is lost. This is just my opinion and I know others may disagree, so I leave it to you decide for yourself and strongly encourage you to read all things warrior to help you along the way.   Since this isn't a history book and I don't want to get bogged down, I am painting in broad stokes; in the back of the book is a suggested reading list. The one constant you find in this book is I will lay stuff out there and encourage you to think, but in the end it is your path and as a warrior you must choose which steps to take.

Here are a few lessons that I have learned (are still learning) along the way. Maybe they will help you on your journey.

Lesson One

Life is difficult.

Dr. Peck starts his book "A Road Less Traveled" off with this theme and it is also a variation on one of the Four Noble Truths. "The Nature of Suffering, birth is suffering, aging is suffering, sickness is suffering, dissociation from the loved is suffering, not to get what one wants is suffering" (www.buddhanet.net).

What does this mean? Don't take difficulties personally. Setbacks and disappointments visit us all. It is not the difficulties that define us as a person but how we respond to them. I guess the silly old sayings "life's a bitch" or "shit happens; get over it" really have a much deeper meaning than we think about. Who do you know that doesn't have some misfortune or difficulties in their lives?

The lesson here is to acknowledge that it's not personal (although for argument's sake one could remind us of Karma), and how we choose to face these setbacks and challenges. Do we wallow in self pity, do we give up or do we gather ourselves and find strength in our virtues and beliefs? We may not be able to control anything in this world, but the one thing we will always have control over is the way we react to whatever life throws at us.

Lesson Two

Live in the NOW.

Yesterday is a memory and tomorrow is just a dream. What we have is the now; learn to live in the moment. Focus on what is happening right now, feel it with all your senses. Some of us are stuck in yesterday and live with regrets and longing. Others live hoping and dreaming of the future without properly preparing for the wanted outcome. (In no way am I advocating not preparing for the future, any good warrior would be planning ahead. We must all have an action plan, but that is another lesson.)

How many people do you know that are reliving their high school glory, lost in that golden yesterday? How many people do you know dream away the daydreaming of that perfect tomorrow? How many people sleepwalk through their days forgetting that they could end at any minute? We have been blessed with the now. Enjoy it! Live each day as if it is your last. Take inventory of the beauty around you, the wonder of the sunrise, the smells of nature, the caress of the wind, the arms of a loved one.

Learning to live in the now means remembering that every action may be your last, walk your virtues and mind your manner. Wouldn't it be a shame if your last action was one that you would not be proud of?

Lesson Three

Good things happen when you're aggressive.

Yes, I know you read this earlier, but it bears repeating. Have you ever heard about a sports team playing on their heels? Or watch a football team blow a game playing prevent defense? There is a saying about how a good defense is a good offence and it's true, you can't win if you don't attack. We are not talking about being rude or having an inappropriate behavior, we are talking about living life to the fullest. There is an old saying: "it is better to live one day as a lion then a thousand as a lamb." Be aggressive in planning your goals and working toward achieving them. Don't be a bystander in life. Always be working toward a goal, toward bettering yourself. Be active always; if you're not moving ahead you are moving backwards. To the victor go the spoils!

Lesson Four

Strike through the target.

Whether you are striking a board or setting goals you must go beyond the target. The power is in executing through the target. Set goals in life that challenge you and take you out of your comfort zone. We must constantly look to improve ourselves.

We didn't stop in grade school once we learned our ABCs or simple addition and subtraction. We took what we had learned and applied them as tools for our next goal. Nothing has changed since the class room. I think many times in life we have dreams, but we fail to turn those dreams into goals with solid action plans to help breakdown the larger goal into smaller road-sign goals that help us achieve the overall desired result.

If one wants to run the Boston marathon, they don't just enter the event. It takes months—even years!—to properly prepare. You would need to start with smaller goals. Run a mile a day for 2 weeks, then work up to 3 miles, 5 miles etc.

So once again it's about knowing your target and preparing yourself to strike though it, and then working to go just a little beyond the goal. If I strike a board and I focus on hitting the board it may very well stop me. If I train and focus on striking through the board, then my success rate jumps up considerably. So set goals, work to achieve them and strike through them.

How many times does growth come just on the other side of pain or discomfort? Think in terms of working out. You want a better body you must put the effort in. When working out do you stop at the first sign of discomfort? Discomfort not pain (that could be a problem and one would stop and consult a doctor). So you are working out, doing chest, let's say bench press. You want to grow and shape your body you must put on enough weight to challenge yourself and you can't stop at the first signs of struggle, you must push past that if you want results. If you can press the weight 6 times without effort then it is the 7th and 8th times that pushes you towards new growth, of striking beyond the target...same with college classes, training programs, etc.—anything that challenges you to strike beyond the target.

Lesson Five

Change yourself, change the world.

Oscar Wilde once said "If not me, who? If not now, when?" That's a sentiment that I try to live by, and it goes along with lesson two. I know this is a quote by Gandhi and it really hits to the core of a warrior. As warriors we are agents of change. We cannot sit and talk about changing things without action, you cannot do spell work to help find a job then not get out and put applications in and get your resume out. You want to change something, you, your situation, your job, relationship then, again, I say take inventory, develop an action plan and do it…

You have the power to change everything. First you should take a good hard look in the mirror, does the situation call for change or do you need to change your attitude and perception about it? I cannot express enough how important attitude is in shaping your life. I know this first hand because I struggle with negativity. I fight the inner demons and try to remain positive. It makes a big difference. Like attracts like, and if you are wallowing in negativity then you will most likely have self-fulfilling prophesies.

So change yourself, and remember any activity takes 21 days to become a habit. Need to lose weight (Gods know I do)? Then start working out. Need a better job? Start by evaluating your skill set and improving your marketability in the job market. Then, get a resume together and begin the process. Need to eat better? Start one meal at a time. Every act you do resonates out to the world around you. You have tremendous influence on people and your environment. So don't complain about things. Make an effort to change things, start with yourself, influence those around you, and make a commitment to better the world.

Lesson Six

Economy of force

I know this may sound contradictive to some of the other lessons but what it really comes down to balance. Yes we need to be aggressive in life and strike through the targe,t but we also need to listen to the rhythms of nature and our bodies. You have all heard the saying about "all work and no play". It's easy to get caught up in something and have tunnel vision, but it's not healthy. I see it in ADF daily where the person's entire world is wrapped up with their grove. I know because I too have this problem. Then I look around and realize that I haven't seen my relatives for weeks, or that the garage is a mess and all those home improvement projects continue to be forgotten.

Economy of force means understanding balance and time management. My wife has a great program called "Fly Lady" that helps with this. It shows how just 15 minutes a day dedicated to an activity can create a world of difference.

Whether it is going through the piles of mail or a daily devotional, it is worth it. What one must remember is to use enough force to get the job done and no more. One must learn when and how much force to apply. You strike beyond the target but just beyond. Make sure you leave time to do the things you need to, or want to. Most importantly take time for you.

● ● ● ● ●

I hope these lessons help you. I know every once in a while I need to reread them myself. These are just six lessons. Add to them with your own or throw them away and write your own, but learning must include reflection and an adjustment to our understanding. As we learn more information, we must alter our perspective to reflect the new data. Like an operating system in your computer, we must always be looking for the newest updates.

"The bravest are surely those who have the clearest vision of what is before them, glory and danger alike, and yet notwithstanding, go out to meet it."

~Thucydides

Chapter Eight

Pulling it all together

Many words ago at the beginning of the book, I introduced the idea of the Warrior Way. I then proceeded to take you on a "long a winding road," but as the song goes, the road ends where it begins. I did not, maybe could not, go over everything that I have learned over the years, nor did I offer up dogma or doctrine. I simple shared with you an idea, a kernel, a seed; now what you do with that seed is up to you. My hope is for you to plant it in your heart and tend it with love and care and let it grow.

I think the essence of the warrior is forgotten in today society. The greed and what about me attitude has left us empty inside. I think the warrior archetype has been given an unfairly bad rap. The true essence of warrior-hood is needed now more than ever. It is time to us to return to the Warrior Way. It is time for us to stand up and take inventory of our actions and the actions of our government, our churches, our children. It is time for us to be active. Proactive, engaged!

Like a ripple in the water, your actions more outward into the world and have an effect on those around you. Use this book to level your coffee table if nothing else, but if it encourages you to action, then it has done its job. I hope you walk away with more. If all else has failed you then, I encourage you to look at the three strands of fabric that weave the tapestry of my work: service, honor and balance.

I am painting in broad strokes. In the back of the book is the suggested reading list. I state again: The one constant you find in this book is that I have laid stuff out there and encouraged you to think, but in the end it is your path and as a warrior you must choose which steps to take.

Appendix 1: Rituals

Native American Style Warrior Ritual (non ADF)

To the Spirits of East, to the mighty Eagle, to the new dawn, and new perspectives, I call to you Spirits and ask that you join my circle this day.

To the Spirits of South, to the rising Phoenix, the noonday sun and transformation, I call to you Spirits and ask that you join my circle this day.

To the Spirits of West, to the watchful Crane, the setting sun and reflection, I call to you Spirits and ask that you join my circle this day.

To the Spirits of North, to the silent Owl, the star filled night and intuition; I call to you Spirits and ask that you join my circle this day.

May the four winds carry my voice to all the creatures of the world. I stand here today to ask for help upon my path.

Grandfathers, Grandfathers, I call to you in praise and thanks. You who taught me sacrifice and responsibility may I never forget your face.

Grandmothers, Grandmothers, I call to you in praise and thanks. You who taught me love and compassion may I never forget you face.

To my tribe I pledge myself this day. May I walk as a warrior in service to those around me. May I be a helping hand to those in need, may I be a shoulder to those who struggle. May I comfort the old and feebly to the best of my ability.

To my tribe I pledge myself this day. May I walk as a guardian in honor to those who have fallen. May I be a warrior of me word, may I guard those around me from harm. May I be a living example of my virtues for the tribe to see.

To my tribe I pledge myself this day. May I walk as a steward to the world around me. May I walk gently on our Mother Earth, may I remember nature's spiral dance and my place within it. To all creatures great and small may I remember your lessons and value in the web of life.

To the Great Spirit, may I remember that I am but a blade of grass, the breath of the buffalo, the noontime shadow and a ripple on the water. May my actions and deeds live forever on the wind, whispered in the trees, and echoing in the hearts of my tribe.

I give to this offering to all that walk the red road with me. May my days be red and blue.

With a song in my heart I give to you Great Spirit. I give to you my ancestors. I give to you my nature allies. I give to you the four winds. To the Spirits of North, West, South and East I give to you. I stand at the Sacred Center and give sacrifice and praise. May I walk in service, honor and balance. So be it.

And now having given to the powers, I call out one last time to the Spirits of the circle. Spirits of North, West, South and East, Spirits above and below until again we meet in sacred space may there be peace between us. This rite has ended.

Veteran's Day Memorial Solitary Ritual

I never do out-dwellers at home due to both respect for my house wights and the warders of our house. (Thor and Brigit) I use Garanus (Crane) as my gate keeper and animal ally but you can use any gate keeper you wish.

I call out to Garanus, Mighty Crane

Walker between the worlds,

But beholden to none

Totem guide, grove mate

One foot on land, one in the water, with your head raised to the sky

Join your magic with mine, ward and aid me mighty Crane, let fire of my heart shrine connect to the fire before me and open as a gate.

Let my blood that courses through me mingle with the waters in the well before me and open as a gate.

Help me to connect myself to the sacred center, becoming a scared pillar between the worlds.

Let the gates be open!

[Offering made to gate keeper]

First I thank the Mother Earth

All that I am and all that I have

Is because of you

You cradle me in your bosom

You clothe me, feed me and keep me

May I walk softly and leave only foot prints

[Offering made]

Ancestors walk with me today and always,

Thank you for your lessons and sacrifices.

To the well I give offerings and ask my ancestors

Those of blood and bone, those of spirit and faith,

Those who have blazed the trails before me so that I may walk easier,

I praise and thank you.

Hail the Ancestors.

[Offering made]

Nature Spirits walk with me today and always,

Thank you for your lessons and sacrifices.

To the tree I give offerings and ask my Nature Spirits

Those of stone and soil, tree and leaf, blood and bone,

Those who dance the spiral dance with me so that I may walk in balance,

I praise and thank you.

Hail the Nature Spirits

[Offering made]

Shining Ones walk with me today and always,

Thank you for your wisdom and blessings.

To the fire I give offerings and ask my Shining Ones

Those of my grove, those of my hearth, and those of my heart.

You who light the way with your brilliance, may I walk in my virtues.

I praise and thank you.

Hail the Shining Ones

[Offering made]

To the Kindred three,

For all the blessings I thank thee

May my voice resound in the well.

May my voice echo through the trees.

May my voice carry on the fire.

I stand before you mighty, noble, ancient ones,

Not broken or on bent knee

But standing tall and free.

Thankful for the blessings you have given me.

May I walk in honor, balance, and service

May my actions be just,

My thoughts pure.

Hail and glory to the Kindreds

To all those gathered I stand here today,

To honor those who have sacrificed.

The first candle I light is for those who have fallen.

All those who made the ultimate sacrifice,

And to those you left behind.

The second candle I light for all those who have served.

I yell praises to you for your sacrifice.

To all those who made it home, THANK YOU.

And this third candle I light is for those still serving.

May it be a beacon in the night.

May it shine brightly and show you the way home!

And now I raise my horn (glass) and honor all the veterans.

Thank you for the service and sacrifice that you have made for your country and communities. Words cannot express my gratitude...

Hail the veterans!

[Drink]

To the Kindreds I ask that you watch over those still serving. I again praise the Kindreds and thank them for joining me at my fire.

Praise and thanks to the Ancestors.

Praise and thanks to the Nature Spirits

Praise and thanks to the Shining Ones.

To my mother, help to remember the cycles of nature

And to be a good steward for the future.

Praise and thanks to the Earth Mother.

Now Garanus, Crane-kin, I call on you once again. I thank you for your lessons and guidance mighty one, and ask once again join your magic with mine.

Let me withdraw back into myself closing the gate, let the well be only water and yet let me be renewed for having it washed over me, and let the fire of my heart shrine burn down to red flickering coals ever ready for the next time...let the gates be closed!

Weekly Blessing Ritual

We come together on this day for a Weekly Blessing Rite, to acknowledge the blessing s in our lives and to continue to build the *ghosti* relationship with the kindred of this Grove. As always we call out to the Earth Mother.

Earth Mother, Great Mother, you who support and nourish us, you who feed us, and shelter us. All that we are, is because of you, may our footsteps by light upon you. Earth Mother, accept our sacrifice.

Now let us look in our heart shrines and feel the flames of our piety. Kindle those flames in your mindseye, breathe deeply now and feel that flames grow, and begin to flicker, glowing a bright orange. Now join me as we intone Awen three times, each time let the powers of inspiration grow within you. Feel the power flickering down your arms and legs and up to the crown of your head, spilling out to fountain around you.

Awen (x3)

This is the power of your piety; each time you sacrifice and kindle this fire it grows stronger in you. It can recharge you, protect you, and shield you. Let this fire burn away all that is unwanted and unneeded. Let it illuminate your soul and your mind. Let it shine into all the corners of your being. Let nothing be hidden from this light.

And now Children of Earth once again look into yourself and find the cauldron of your soul. In the cauldron are the waters of your potential. Your essence, your life-force; these waters hold the DNA of all your ancestors, handed down generation to generation. Feel these waters welling up and over flowing out of the cauldron, flowing through you, pouring down your arms and legs, out your mouth and eyes, up and over you flowing and mixing with the flames of your piety.

Breathe deep and allow these two powers to mix in you and around you. Exhale and see the steam release from you, from the others around you, see the steam cool on the air and create a mist about you, rising up to the heavens and down to the earth…stand here alive and full of energy yet grounded and steady.

Allow these mists of magic to swirl around you and close off the mundane world. See the mist grey and colorless yet alive and full of color. Formless yet with shapes that form and dissipate around you. Listen closely and you hear the waves gently splashing as it hits the shores…see the waters thru the mist…see the Druid's moon reflecting in the waters, these are the deep cosmic waters…look now into the distance. Look there beyond the ninth wave, in the distance, riding in on the wind, Garanus, Crane. Flying to you, to settle here in the mist of magic, one foot on the shore, one foot in the water, an eye toward the sky…sit now with the crane. Join with the crane, feel you heat beat match the rhythm of the crane…join your power, your magic with his (hers), feel the power of earth, sea and sky and together open the gates to the sacred center…

Let the fire open as a gate

Let the well open as a gate

Let the Tree hold fast the Way Between.

Open the Gates!

[Make your standard Kindred Offerings]

Garanus, friend, warder, watcher, teacher, fellow traveler, although we work together this day we also give you praise and sacrifice. Garanus, Crane-kin for the lessons that you teach us, for the blessing you give us, we give your this sacrifice.

And now that we have given, we ask what lessons oh, noble, mighty, shining ones do you have for us. Until we met again what lesson should we reflect on?

[Pull Your Omen]

Thank you Kindred and Mighty Crane for this blessing, we will reflect upon this lesson until once again we met at the sacred center.   And so Children of the Earth we have given to the Kindred and they in turn have given to us. Let the blessing of the Shining ones now well up from below, shine down from above, see the cup of magic as it changes and is filled with the waters of life…once again see the flames of piety reflective in these waters and know that they are charged with the power of the kindred…behold the waters of life…

[Drink your blessings]

Again breathe deep, feel these blessings as they grow within you. Mixing and charging the waters within you, feeding the flames in your heart shrine…

[Thank the Kindreds]

Garanus, we once again call to you crane-kin, let us finish what we have started. Join again your magic to ours and…

Let the fire be just a flame

Let the well be just water

Let all be as it was before, save for the magic we have made

Let the Gates be closed!

Garanus, Friend, we thank you for assistance in our work and in our lives. Animal ally, always watching, always warding – we thank you!

Children of the Earth, close your eyes and once again feel the power within you…allow the mist of magic to dissipate, feel the waters of potential draw inward, returning to the cauldron of your soul, see the flames of your piety reflective on the water…now see the flames begin to die down…slowing burning out until there is just a glowing embers in your heart shrine…ready and waiting for the next time you feed the flames…and now stand tall and refreshed from your work…feel the earth beneath you. Steady and grounding…bend down and release any leftover energy to her, allowing it to sink into her soft and gentle, like a kiss…

[Thank the Earth Mother and close your rite]

Group Warrior Sumble (ADF style)

Process to hall — stop

Guardian Prayer

I stand firm with the Earth beneath me.

I stand tall with the Sky above me.

I stand strong with the Sea around me.

With the power of the Earth, Sea and Sky,

 I stand ready.

I am aided by the might of the Kindred

I am a guardian for this grove (hall)

 and stand ever vigilant

Prayer for Peace

May there be peace in the North, in the East,

in the South and in the West

May there be peace from above and below

May there be peace among us.

May the Ancestors remind us of our history

 and council our action and deeds.

May the Nature Spirits remind us of our

responsibilities and council our hearts and

minds.

May the Shining Ones remind us of our
potential and council our thoughts and
dreams.
May our work be in honor, service and
balance.

[Note: Procession waits outside of hall and the Lady of the Hall steps forward]

Lady: "Welcome all to the hall those who walk together under the banners of their grove and those who stand alone but together with us all."

[All enter hall: Groves announced as they enter. Solitaries enter last and welcomed by all.]

Host (Lord of the Hall): "Hail and welcome all to the hall. Has everyone who wishes to enter the hall done so?"

Lone Warrior: "NO, there are many who have fallen and many, who serve. Let this light burn bright in memory and in honor to their service and sacrifice, hail the warriors!"

The Hall: "Hail the warriors!"

[Lone Warrior walks in and places lantern on main altar]

Earth Mother:

All Hail the mother Earth.

Thank you for all your blessings.

You who hold us in your arms, who feed us, clothe us and keep us.

All Mother, Our Mother

We give you praise and honor.

[Offering made]

Inspiration:

[Sing]

Powers of Inspiration

We are calling out to you

Kindle the fire in our heart

Inspire everything we do

May our actions by just

May our words ring true

Powers of Inspiration

We praise you.

[Offering made]

Meditation:

Listen to your breathing, quiet your mind, think of your thoughts as background noise on a radio and turn them down. Listen to your body, feel your body.

Take inventory of yourself, relaxing, breathing deep, in....out...in...out. Feel the weight of your arms as they are hanging by your sides...

Breathe in deeply and hold it for a second; then slowly exhale...slowly and completely. Breathe in and out, feel your legs and feet and wiggle your toes...

Take another deep breath, and hold it before slowly releasing it...ahhhhhhh.

Feel you heartbeat, listen to the soft beating that courses the blood through your body...

Relax and feel that rhythm. Roll your neck and relax, allow your body to go deeper...relaxing and listening to your own breathing...again take a deep breath...hold it....and slowly release, it pushing at the end until all the breath is out...

Now in your minds-eye, imagine a seaside...paint a picture in your mind of waves as they gently flow onto the beach and then just as easily recede back out...

Hear that sound of the surf…that gentle whooshing sound of the waves as they meet the sand…and that sound joins in the rhythm of your heartbeat. Feel the solid ground beneath your feet and allow yourself to dig into the sand and take root into the earth. Feel your heartbeat join now with the heartbeat of the Earth Mother…draw strength from her…

Hear the sound of birds and smell the salt in the air…continue to breathe deep…in and out…

Feel the wind and sun on your face…allow yourself to enjoy the moment…feel the warmth of the sun, relax and just breathe…

Allow your cares to flow away on the waves…in and out like your breathing…as the waves take your troubles and concerns away, feel the wind blow away doubt and negativity. Breathe deep and relax, be at ease with yourself…

The sunlight that warms your face penetrates you and energizes you. Warms you to the core…let that warmth wash over you…now just be…relaxed, energized.

Preparing the Sacred Center

Warrior Gateway, Written by Emerald

Bard "Warriors now hold fast in your minds the image of a patron warrior deity, a hero or courageous ancestor close to your heart, or a warrior ally from amongst the worldly spirits. See them, hear them, and remember how it feels to be in their presence...Now, as one voice, we call to them"

[Note: Simultaneously, warriors call out the name of their Gatekeeper]

Bard: "Again!" (They do it again.)

Bard: "Again." (They do it a final time.)

Bard: "Warriors we call draw near.

To Warriors standing here.

From the halls and palaces of the realm above, on high in the starry sky. . ."

Warriors: "Warriors we call draw near, to Warriors standing here!"

Bard: "From the fields and halls of the realm below, rebirth in the well of earth"

Warriors: "Warriors we call draw near, to Warriors standing here!"

Bard: "From within our world in the middle realm, world of green seen and unseen"

Warriors: "Warriors we call draw near, to Warriors standing here!"

Bard: "Warriors of the Kins! Warriors of the Folk! We stand close to each other; only the gates between the worlds stand between us now. Together we focus our magic and might that our power will freely flow this night."

[Offering made to Gatekeeper, bard bangs staff three times]

All: "The gates are open!"

Honoring and Inviting the Three Kindred

Hail to our Ancestors.

You who have become before us.

You of blood and spirit, mind and body.

You who have taught us the lessons of love and honor.

We give you praise and honor.

Hail the Ancestors! (Warriors repeat)

[Offering made]

Hail to the Land Spirits

To our brother and sisters,

Of rock and stone, tree and twig,

Animal allies, totem guides, and you of fur, feather, scale and skin

You who remind us that we am but one in the world not above or below but beside, in the circle…

We give you praise and honor

Hail the Nature Spirits! (Warriors repeat)

[Offering made]

Hail to the Shining Ones

To our matrons and patrons

To those of hearth, heart, kith and kin.

You who illuminate our dreams and lives.

You who shine down your love and blessings!

We give you praise and honor.

Hail the Shining Ones! (Warriors repeat)

[Offering made]

To the mighty, noble kindred; we praise you for all your blessings. For the blessings of health and happiness, enough wealth to survive, for protecting our friends and family we honor you. May we walk in honor, balance, and service.

Establishing Frith Stead

Host: "Hail Tyr, Great Sky father, Guardian of Order, God of the Thing. You who walks with us, teaches us and reminds us to be true to heart, and to act with honor and frith. We hail and honor you. You who sacrificed yourself for the good of the tribe; let our words ring true, our actions be just, may we remember that we can disagree without being disagreeable. May this ritual be about celebrating friendships and making memories. May we long remember the friendship and fellowship that we have created in this hall. Let all remember that this Frith-stead has been raised. Hail Tyr!"

All: "Hail Tyr!"

[This begins the community bloat – one round or three depending on time and energy of hall.]

Charging the horn.

This is usually done by the Lady of the Hall with words from the heart and making a hammer sign over the horn.

1st round – Gods/Goddesses

2nd round – Ancestors, Totems, and Heroes

3rd round – Toast, boast and Oaths

Notes: Oaths are to be taken very seriously; it is accepted and expected that oaths be defined and challenged. I usually place oath sickle around the neck of those taking oath. I have seen others have them place their hands on the sickle. I say something like...

"Oaths are always a sacred thing but oaths taken in sumble take on even more meaning. All those gathered here to witness this oath are also tied to this oath for an oath spoken over the horn of Wyrd will bind our Wyrd together. Do not oath lightly; is it your intent to oath?"

If yes then I say "Then proceed with your oath" I will often time ask questions and for clarification of details and will also set up payment/sacrifice for failed oath. Once the oath is taken I ask the hall, "And so you have heard this oath, taken and explained do you accept this oath." If no one challenges the oath I say

"Then you have made you oath, it is between you and your Gods, witnessed by the hall, if you are to fail in your oath then may the sky fail down upon you, may the land crumble beneath you and may the seas swallow you whole. "

If no then we continue to discuss and define the oath until all are happy.

Waters of Life/Return Flow

Unlike most ADF rituals the waters of life is concurrent with the sumble, as we praise the Kindreds they in return bless us by strengthening our relationships with the Kindreds and each other. I usually say something like

"And so my friends we have come together in sacred space we have shared our hearts and our beliefs. We have praised and sacrificed to the Kindreds, we have prayed with a good fire. The blessings we receive tonight are infused in the mead. They linger on your lips from the shared horn. Allow tonight's work to take shape in our hearts and echo in our work and lives. We have been blessed with fellowship, and we have strengthened our community. Let us now take omens asking what more the kindred have for us on this wonderful night…"

Omen

The seer for this rite will ask three questions:

Have our offerings been accepted?

What do the Powers offer us in return?

What further needs do the Powers have of us?

Thanking

In reverse order we thank all the Kindred.

Closing the Gates

Reverse Opening - use same images

Thank Inspiration.

Thank Earth Mother

Ending:

"From the Earth, to us, to the Gods, from the Gods, to us, to the Earth. We have done as our ancestors have done, and as our children will do; go now, children of the Earth, in peace and blessings. The ritual has ended. So be it"

Appendix 2: Recommended Reading and Resources

It would be impossible to list every book that I have read and that has influenced me and my opinions over the last forty some years. These books are the well-worn books that are on my bookstand or more likely piled beside by side of the bed. The book was written in several drafts and through 4 different computers, and pulled from my own ADF clergy training etc so it is possible that I have forgotten someone. If I have then please forgive me, to every book I have ever read and for anyone who has put pen to paper or clicked away at the typewriter or computer you have my profound respect.

A Book of Pagan Prayer

By Ceisiwr Serith

Weiser Books (May 1, 2002)

A Brief History of the Druids (The Brief History)

By Peter Berresford Ellis

Running Press (April 10, 2002)

A History of Pagan Europe

By Prudence Jones and Nigel Pennick

Barnes and Noble 1995.

Blood Rites: Origins and History of the Passions of War

By Barbara Ehrenreich

Owl Books (May 15, 1998)

Bonewits's Essential Guide to Druidism

By Isaac Bonewits

Citadel Press. 2006.

Celtic Heritage

By Alwyn Rees and Brinley Rees

Thames and Hudson; Revised edition (May 1, 1989)

Chop Wood, Carry Water

By Rick Fields

Tarcher; 1st edition (December 1, 1984)

Comparative Mythology

By Jaan Puhvel

The Johns Hopkins University Press (August 1, 1989)

Creation of the Sacred

By Walter Burkert

Harvard University Press. 1996.

Deep Ancestors: Practicing the Religion of the Proto-Indo-Europeans

By Ceisiwr Serith

ADF Publishing

From Private Practice to Public Ritual: Ritual Foundations I

By Michael Dangler, James Dillard and others

Garanus Publishing 2011 [Link]

Full Contact Magick: A Book of Shadows for the Wiccan Warrior

Kerr Cuhulain

Llewellyn Publications (September 8, 2002)

Gods and Myths of Northern Europe

By H.R. Ellis Davidson

Penguin Books (January 3, 1965)

In Search of the Indo-Europeans

By J. P. Mallory

Thames & Hudson (April 1, 1991)

King, Warrior, Magician, Lover: Rediscovering the Archetypes of the Mature Masculine

By: Robert Moore (Author), Douglas Gillette

HarperOne; Reprint edition (August 16, 1991)

Neo Pagan Rites

By Isaac Bonewits

Llewellyn Publications. 2007.

Our Own Druidy :An Introduction to Ár nDraíocht Féin and the Druid Path.

ADF Press. 2009.

Our Troth Vol 1.

By Kveldulf Gundarsson

The Troth/BookSurge.2006.

Pagan Celtic Britain

By Anne Ross

Academy Chicago Publishers (August 30, 2005)

Sacred Fire, Holy Well

By Ian Corrigan

Tredara Hearth Publishing. 2006.

Taking Up The Runes: A Complete Guide To Using Runes In Spells, Rituals, Divination, And Magic

By Diana L Paxson

Weiser Books (April 20, 2005)

The Archetypes and The Collective Unconscious (Collected Works of C.G. Jung Vol.9 Part 1)

By C. G. Jung

Princeton University Press; 2 edition (August 1, 1981)

The Code of the Warrior in History, Myth, and Everyday Life

By Rick Fields

Harpercollins (October 1991)

The Fire On Our Hearth: Second Edition: A Devotional of Three Cranes Grove, ADF

By Rev. Michael J. Dangler, James Dillard and others

Garanus Publishing 2009 [Link]

The Horse, the Wheel, and Language: How Bronze-Age Riders from the Eurasian Steppes Shaped the Modern World

By David W. Anthony

Princeton University Press; Reprint edition (July 26, 2010)

The Solitary Druid

By Rev. Robert Lee "Skip" Ellison

Citadel Press Books. 2005.

The Warrior Within: Accessing the Warrior in the Male Psyche

By Robert L. Moore (Author), Douglas Gillette

Avon Books (P) (November 1993)

Trance-portation: Learning to Navigate the Inner World
By Diana L. Paxson
Weiser Books (November 1, 2008)

Wiccan Warrior: Walking a Spiritual Path in a Sometimes Hostile World
By Kerr Cuhulain
Llewellyn Publications (March 2000)

ADF Articles and information from adf.org

Appendix 3: Where To Find Us!

The Magical Druid
Spiritual Resource Center

http://www.magicaldruid.com/

GARANUS PUBLISHING

http://www.lulu.com/garanus

Three Cranes Grove, ADF
PO Box 3264
Columbus, OH 43210